AWARDS for *"Deer in My Garden, Vol. 1"*

USA Book News Book Awards: "Best Gardening Book, 2006"

Independent Publisher: "Highlighted Title" October 2006

Writers Notes Magazine: 2007 Eric Hoffer Award in nonfiction

The New York Book Festival, 2007: Honorable mention in nonfiction

Northern CA Publishers & Authors, 2007: Best First Book, Best Exterior Cover, and silver in Best Book

The Hollywood Book Festival, 2007: Honorable mention in non-fiction

REVIEWS of "*Deer in My Garden, Vol. 1*"

"*We're not exaggerating when we say that* Deer in My Garden *might save you hundreds or even thousands of dollars in plant replacement costs... Carolyn Singer has managed to outdo many horticultural researchers and cooperative extension workers in term of gathering, organizing, and disseminating material that will be extraordinarily valuable to many gardeners.*"
Greg & Pat Williams, HortIdeas, May 2006

"*...a superbly presented and profusely illustrated introduction for the novice gardener and a welcome reference for the experienced horticulturalist... Authoritative, superbly organized, and thoroughly 'user friendly',* Deer in My Garden *is a seminal and core addition to personal, professional, academic, and community library Gardening Resources reference collections and supplemental reading lists.*"
James Cox, Editor-in-Chief
The Midwest Book Review, October 2006

"*...the most intelligent and complete book on the topic available...*"
Jim Barnes, Editor
Independent Publisher Online, December 2006

"*The listings offer some well-seasoned gardening experience in a concise and usable format that any gardener will appreciate.*"
Lynette L. Walther
The Camden Herald (MaineCoastNOW.com)

"*After nearly three decades managing Foothill Cottage Gardens nursery and developing demonstration gardens around her home and nursery, Carolyn Singer has more than enough credentials to write this book. Anyone gardening with deer should read this one.*"

Richard G. Turner Jr., Editor
Pacific Horticulture
October/November/December 2007

DEER IN MY GARDEN

VOLUME 2: GROUNDCOVERS & EDGERS

by Carolyn Singer

ABOUT THE AUTHOR

Carolyn Singer has been gardening since she was a young child. Early horticultural lessons were from her parents, first in Berkeley, and then in Sebastopol, California. Extended family members in Sonoma County were all gardeners, adding to Carolyn's enthusiastic connection with the earth.

Gardening in the Denver area for eight years and camping in the beautiful Rocky Mountains were influential in her growing interest in rock gardening.

For the past 30 years, on her property in the Sierra Nevada foothills near Grass Valley, California, she has been testing hundreds of perennials for their performance and deer-resistance.

Carolyn's perennial nursery, Foothill Cottage Gardens, and display gardens in Grass Valley were open to the public for 25 years. Her nursery was recognized nationally in publications ("Organic Gardening", "Fine Gardening", "Country Gardening", and "Sunset") and in "Taylor's Guide to Specialty Nurseries".

Garden classes have been held every year. She has also taught at Sierra College. Students continue to enjoy her propagation classes, held several times each summer in her garden, to propagate from the huge assortment of plants.

Carolyn writes a garden column for her local paper, "The Union" in Grass Valley, California. She has published garden articles in "Fine Gardening", "Garden Gate", "Better Homes and Gardens Special Interest Publications", and "Sierra Heritage" magazine.

Carolyn's rock garden, which is the inspiration for many of the perennials in Volume 2, has been featured on HGTV's Paul James, "Gardening By the Yard". When they filmed the segment about gardening with rocky soil, Carolyn's garden was a perfect site.

Her designs have been published in "Home Landscaping California Region", by Roger Holmes and Lance Walheim (published by Creative Homeowner Press, 2001). Her work is also mentioned in Judith M. Taylor's "Tangible Memories, Californians and Their Gardens, 1800-1850" (published 2003).

In 1995 she contributed to the updated Time-Life "Complete Gardener: Perennials". She is a member of the Perennial Plant Association (PPA), the American Rock Garden Society, and the California Native Plant Society (CNPS). She has received the honor of "Lifetime University of California Master Gardener".

ACKNOWLEDGMENTS

PHOTO BY SEAN MCMILLIN

Recognition of my grandchildren is first. I thank Marcus, who at age three concluded that his grandmother should grow "yucky flowers" because "the deer wouldn't eat yucky flowers!" And I thank Carina, who has always felt that my rock garden was a special place. At age five, she told the daughter of a nursery customer: "Come see my grandma's magic garden!" She even helps me weed this garden!

The enthusiastic response to "Deer in My Garden, Vol. 1" has inspired me to write Volume 2. Thank you to all of my clients, customers, students, friends, and family for your support! Also, I want to express my appreciation to those new clients who were willing to wait for fall and even winter landscaping, while I spent the summer of 2007 gardening and writing this second volume.

While my own garden has been a testing ground, it is my many landscape clients who have broadened my awareness of how each plant performs in a given microclimate.

I wish to thank Katy Hight, my friend and graphic designer, for her talent, her flexibility, and her involvement in every phase of production. Her enthusiastic support has meant a lot to me these past two years.

Alicia Berardi of Ivy Photography in Grass Valley has used my rock garden frequently as a setting for her beautiful artwork. I am grateful that my cover photograph was taken by her in this special garden.

I greatly appreciate that my son Sean took time in his busy life to create another beautiful cover design.

Greg and Pat Williams of "HortIdeas" recognized the extensive research that was the basis for Volume 1. Their own publication of horticultural research is a wealth of gardening information, and I feel honored to have had my book reviewed by them in "HortIdeas" in May 2006.

Thank you all!

Deer in My Garden
Volume 2: Groundcovers & Edgers
by Carolyn Singer

Copyright © 2008 by Carolyn Singer
Printed in the United States of America

Garden Wisdom Press
www.gardenwisdompress.com

Cover design: Sean McMillin
Interior design: Katy Hight
Photography: Carolyn Singer

Printed in China through Global Interprint, Santa Rosa, California
Printed on 100% recycled paper with soy inks

Singer, Carolyn.
    Deer in my garden. Vol. 2, Groundcovers & edgers / by
Carolyn Singer. -- 1st ed.
    p. cm. -- (The yucky flower series)
    Includes index.
    ISBN-13: 978-0-9774251-5-0 (print ed.)
    ISBN-10: 0-9774251-5-0 (print ed.)
    ISBN-13: 978-0-9774251-6-7 (PDF ed.)
    ISBN-10: 0-9774251-6-9 (PDF ed.)
    [etc.]

    1. Gardening--Handbooks, manuals, etc. 2. Deer.
    3. Perennials--Diseases and pests--Handbooks, manuals, etc.
    4. Ground cover plants--Diseases and pests--Handbooks,
manuals, etc.   I. Title. II. Series.

SB450.96.S56 2007   635.9'26965
                QBI07-600229

CONTENTS

PLANNING AND PLANTING
IN DEER COUNTRY

Groundcovers are essential to good landscape design. These plants may be used to cover large or small areas, providing a backdrop for a specimen tree, ornamental shrub, ornamental grass, or even a taller perennial. In many landscape situations, the groundcover itself becomes a focal area.

I use the term groundcover in a broad sense, including those plants that spread low to the ground and those that may be three feet in height with a broad spread. In a small garden, perennials under six inches in height are more suitable as groundcovers, while in a larger scale landscape several mounding plants of three to four-foot spread may be massed as an effective groundcover.

There are three common groundcovers I have not included: ivy (*Hedera*), creeping St. Johnswort (*Hypericum calycinum*), and periwinkle (*Vinca*). While all three are deer-resistant, they are also very invasive. Ivy in particular has been extremely damaging to other landscape plants. *Vinca minor* may be used as a shady groundcover in an area where dense coverage is desirable.

Appendix 2 lists deer-resistant shrubs and subshrubs (under three to four feet) that may be used as "groundcovers". The advantage of these taller plants, especially in country gardens, is that they seldom need to be weeded once mature, and may be utilized in areas where seeds from nearby weeds are likely to invade the planted area.

Edgers have been selected as choice plants to use along a path or at the edge of a flower border. Most are restrained in their growth habit. While many of the low groundcovers spread from stolons, vigorously covering open ground, the edgers are chosen because of the limits to their spread. Some of these plants are beautiful as single specimens, and some may be grouped together to form a groundcover.

Groundcovers and edgers are detailed in description, bloom, cultural requirements, seasonal interest, companion plants and landscape use, propagation, and maintenance.

Appendix 2 also includes a listing of very small deer-resistant groundcovers, ideal for edging a walkway, or as single specimens in wall niches.

Deer-resistance of plants described in this volume is based on trials in my own garden and in landscapes I have designed. Information from gardeners in other geographical areas has been invaluable.

There seems to be evidence that the lush growth of plants fertilized with nitrogen (organic or chemical) may be more attractive to the deer. I have compared fertilized "deer-resistant" plants with unfertilized plants. The deer will repeatedly attack the fertilized plant and leave the same plant growing next to it untouched. Since plants purchased in a nursery have been fertilized, it is advisable to protect all new plantings for a few months. In my garden, I most often use wildlife netting, rather than sprays which must be reapplied.

Nomenclature & classification in the plant world is changing as DNA is analyzed, and plants are reclassified based on their genetics. In this volume, genus and species follow the listing in "Hortus Third" or "Index Hortensis". Some species names in these references are capitalized in honor of the person or place from which the name is derived. Named cultivars are indicated in single quotes, and when these names vary in spelling, both are listed. When a plant has more than one common name, all are included. Plants are listed alphabetically by common name in Appendix 1.

A subspecies is indicated by "ssp". The use of "cv" refers to cultivar and "sp." to species.

The classification "species *Narcissus*" includes a group of *Narcissus* of wild origins, naturalized hundreds of years ago. All have been deer-resistant. Species *Crocus* and species *Tulipa* have similar wild origins, and some have been deer-resistant in my garden.

Description is essential for informed selection of plants. While a plant looks "pretty" in a nursery container, this same plant may quickly lose its appeal in your garden if it spreads too vigorously. Knowing how large a plant will be at maturity is also necessary for effective artistic placement in the landscape.

For a large-scale groundcover, the habit of spreading vigorously is desirable, but for a single accent plant or a small-scale groundcover or edging plant, the selected perennial should not be invasive or broad in its spreading habit.

Spread and spreading habit of growth will determine how far apart to place plants for coverage within two to three years.

Description also includes information about leaf and flower color and form.

Cultural requirements includes detailed information about light and soil preferences, and irrigation requirements. Because many of these plants have not been commonly available in the horticultural trade, there may be information lacking regarding specific zones. However, since many of the plants are found at high mountain elevations and they have all been grown by the author, their winter hardiness may be predicted.

Be attentive to the seasonal changes of light in your garden. Light requirements are specified for each plant during the growing season. Plants requiring full sun year-round should not be placed where they will receive shade in winter. Some perennial groundcovers for shade will even tolerate the lower light in winter. However, many shade-loving plants may thrive in the winter sun under a deciduous tree.

Partial shade may be morning sun followed by afternoon shade, or it may be the dappled shade of a deciduous tree. Some trees allow more light under their branches, and some cast very deep shade. The partial shade under the north side of the tree is usually the darker area.

Soil preparation is especially important for groundcovers, since they will not be moved once they are planted. Some are deep-rooted and others shallow-rooted. Growth habit will determine the depth of soil preparation.

Gardeners with sandy soil and those with clay should be adding organic compost to the native soil to increase fertility, and for aeration (especially in clay). The addition of organic phosphorus (soft rock phosphate, rock phosphate, colloidal phosphate) must be done with the initial soil preparation. This amendment is not water-soluble, and is an essential nutrient for root growth and flowering.

Since phosphorus is absorbed in a very narrow pH range (6.5 to 7.5), knowing your soil's acidity is helpful. In acidic soils, the addition of five pounds oystershell per hundred square feet in combination with fifteen to twenty pounds of organic phosphorus, plus one-third compost to two-thirds native soil, is needed for optimal growth. If a plant prefers rich soil, add more compost (to one-half), and use compost as a mulch. Soil in good tilth is fertile and friable, allowing roots to develop.

Oystershell is water-soluble and may be added to the soil surface in any season. In a mature garden, a fall application of five pounds per hundred square feet, plus a renewed layer of compost mulch will reinvigorate growth in the coming spring and summer. Gardeners who do not have acidic soils may use only the compost as a fall application.

Perennials that prefer a "leaner" soil, such as *Artemisia* and *Lavandula,* will exhibit better growth and bloom with one-fourth compost to three-fourths native soil, plus the rock powders. The compost for these rugged perennials should not be high in nitrogen.

Good soil preparation and appropriate mulching usually eliminate the need for supplemental fertilization. Mulches are recommended for each plant, based on their preference. Apply mulches as soon as you have planted, and renew them whenever necessary. Young plantings may be damaged by sun and wind if mulches are not protecting surface roots. Established groundcovers may be mulched annually or every other year with a light application of compost, one-half inch to one inch deep.

In seasons of heavy rainfall, a good mulch prevents soil compaction. In dry periods, a mulched perennial will survive with less irrigation. Each plant is detailed for its irrigation preferences, and the frequency of watering recommended is for a plant that is mulched.

Planting on a slope is challenging. Rains and wind may shift soil and even mulches, exposing surface roots. Placing rocks or a piece of wood on the downside of the plant helps to hold soil and mulch in place initially. Check the mulch regularly for the first year and add more as needed.

Seasonal interest may be highest with bloom, but serious gardeners value their plant choices for changes from season to season. New spring growth is often a different color than older leaves. Even evergreens may have subtle changes in leaf color with winter cold. Seasonal interest may also include the formation of berries or seedheads after bloom, a strong reason to resist deadheading. Even a plant that is deciduous in winter, such as *Cotoneaster* 'Tom Thumb', may have an interesting branching habit that is exquisite with a dusting of snow.

Bloom is what attracts most people to plants, and nurseries know that! Remember that leaf color and form, and the form and texture of the plant, are dominant in the landscape all year. The hue of the stem often plays a colorful role, especially in contrast to leaves.

Climate, microclimates, and weather are all factors determining timing and length of bloom. The warmth of a south-facing slope or reflected heat from a nearby rock may stimulate early bloom. The reduced impact of the sun in an eastern exposure may lengthen the blooming season. Gardeners in cooler coastal regions may enjoy a longer flowering period for some plants.

Because perennials begin bloom at different times in different geographical regions, there is no design suitable for all gardens. Similarly, the length of bloom varies from region to region, and somewhat from year to year.

Deadheading is the removal of faded flowers. For many groundcovers, this is unnecessary maintenance. Following bloom the groundcover will put on a new spurt of growth and cover the faded flowers.

A few of the plants included in this volume may provide material for fresh cut flower arrangements. Always cut early in the morning and placed the stems in warm water to condition the flowers.

Gardeners should seed-save from flowers on mature plants, or allow only a few seeds to mature on a young plant. Plants producing seed will slow in their growth, and, if young, may even show signs of stress.

Companion plants and landscape use includes many ways in which to use each plant in your garden. Some are suitable as individual specimens, some as small-scale groundcovers, and others in large areas.

All companions are selected based on their similar cultural requirements for light exposure, soil fertility, and irrigation frequency. When two plants are growing in proximity, irrigation must meet the needs of the plant requiring more water. While the companion may need less, it is chosen because it will tolerate and even thrive with the more frequent irrigation. For example, prostrate germander (*Teucrium* x *lucidrys* 'Prostratum'), prefers water once every two weeks in my garden. While

English lavender (*Lavandula angustifolia*) thrives in my clay soil with irrigation only once a month, it will tolerate more frequent irrigation where soil drainage is good. Thus, the two are good companions, especially since the germander will creep into the semi-shady area at the base of the lavender.

Effective garden design must consider the eventual size of a plant. A *Cotoneaster* that will spread to five feet is a good choice on a slope, but not as an edging plant in a narrow area close to a walkway. When two different plants are planted close to one another, add the total of the plants' mature spread, divide this figure in half, and plant the center of each plant separated by this distance. Four to five feet between some spreading plants is appropriate spacing.

Landscape use also considers the effect of the foliage. Groundcovers such as *Lamium* may add light to shade gardens with variegated foliage. The dark-green foliage of creeping manzanita (*Arctostaphylos*) may cool a hot slope facing west. In the sun, the contrast of gray and silver foliage is striking combined with the many shades of green.

Some landscape situations are more challenging than others. A north-facing slope receives limited light in winter and often stays wet in areas of heavy rainfall. This same slope may be in full sun in summer. There are plants that will tolerate these extremes. Refer to Appendix 3 for a list of plants that will adapt.

Full-sun western and southern slopes in the intense sunlight of the Sierra Nevada foothills are also difficult. However, there are many beautiful plants that will thrive in this situation. Refer to Appendix 3.

Propagation of some groundcovers is easiest by division. While this may be done during the growing season, plants will be more likely to be shocked, and may not survive. Plants divided from a flat of groundcover will do best when fall planted. If divisions are taken from established plants in the garden, this may be done in fall, winter, or early spring, depending on your climate. Always use a good garden fork to lift plants since it will do less damage to the roots.

Vegetative cuttings may be taken from plants with terminal buds. *Lamium, Lamiastrum, Thymus,* and *Dianthus* are a few examples. The best cuttings are made during the growing season, when growing shoots are not coming into bloom. If possible, choose terminal shoots which have leaf nodes close together, whether opposite or alternate. It is important that the shoot chosen does not have a flowering bud. For example, cuttings from lavender need to be made after the bush has bloomed, and growing shoots show no sign of flower buds.

Work early in the morning, in shade, and take only as many cuttings as you can handle in a few minutes. Cuttings wilt quickly. Do not allow any sun on the cuttings even early in the morning. It is possible to take cuttings from a plant in the sun in the morning, but once taken, protect the cuttings from more sun during the propagation process. If the plant is hydrated, that is, recently watered, cuttings are more likely to be successful.

The best medium for propagation of soft-wood cuttings is one-half perlite to one-half vermiculite. The materials are mixed in a container, and water is added to make a slurry. The material is then moved to the propagation flats. Excess water drains out through the bottom hole. Cells are filled with a slight pressure to ensure that there are no air pockets. Do not press the medium firmly until after the cutting has been inserted. If cuttings are not easily inserted, a toothpick may be used to make a small hole.

Each plant offers a different kind of cutting material: some have many leaf nodes, and a 1-inch cutting will work, while others may have fewer nodes and the longer cutting is necessary. Carefully remove all leaves along the stem except for the few which will remain above the medium. Determine how many leaves your cutting should have. The larger the leaves, the fewer should remain above the medium. Make your final cut below a leaf node. Dip the cutting stem into a rooting hormone (e.g. Rootone), allowing contact with the nodes, and shake off the excess. The cutting should not be wet, or it will hold too much of the rooting hormone. Some cuttings root from the nodes, some from the bottom of the stem where the cut has been made, and some from hairs along the stem.

Work in the shade, and keep your propagated material shaded for two to three weeks. Water with a light spray twice a day or more. If larger leaves still show sign of wilting after a few days, cut them in half. Move the material into bright light but no direct sunlight, and keep it in this exposure for two to three weeks. Remove any flowers that appear, no matter how tiny. At this stage you want the cutting to put all of its energy into growing roots.

After a few weeks, your cuttings should be rooted. Some take longer than others. Cuttings from gray or silver-leafed perennials need to be removed from conditions of high humidity (misting) as soon as they have rooted. Yellowing of leaves will indicate that they are receiving too much moisture.

Cut back the elongated terminal bud to stimulate root growth, and pot up the young starts into containers with a good potting mix. Your planting mix should not be hot, or high in nitrogen. If it is, it may kill these tender young starts. No fertilizing is necessary until plants have shown substantial growth. A container mix that works for young cuttings as well as for perennials that will be grown in a container for a year or more should include compost, vermiculite, perlite, and rock powders.

Young plants may be grown outside through the winter, or within the protection of a cold frame in very cold climates. A row cover, such as Tufbell, may be used to protect the young plants from winter cold when grown outside. However, if plants have been propagated earlier in the summer, and planted as soon as their roots develop, they will have grown enough by fall and will not need winter protection.

Propagation from seed is recommended only when it is an easy method for increasing plant supplies, or the only way to obtain a treasured plant. Sow fresh seed whenever possible; older seed may not germinate, even when it has been stored correctly in cool and dry conditions. Some seed is very fine and should be sown on the surface of the planting medium, since the seed will need light to germinate. This is especially true for plants that self-sow. In my rock garden, seeds often scatter into the gravel paths. I have discovered that this is frequently an ideal seedbed! The young seedlings are moved as soon as I notice them.

Fall and early spring are good seasons for sowing seeds. Sometimes seed sown in the fall will not germinate until spring because it requires stratification, or cold treatment, to break the dormancy of the seed. Duplicating the natural stratification of winter cold by using your refrigerator may actually damage the seed embryo. Modern frost-free refrigerators dehydrate the seed. If you use this method of stratification, mix the seed with moistened vermiculite, seal the mix in a plastic bag, and allow two to three weeks of cold treatment in the refrigerator before sowing outside.

Groundcovers that trail offer an opportunity for propagating by layering. Spread compost under a trailing stem. Anchor the stem close to a leaf node with a landscape staple. Add more compost on top of the anchored section. Fabric held in place by landscape staples or rocks will prevent the compost from shifting. When this section has rooted, it may be cut off and planted. If the section is more than six inches in length, it may need to be cut back to encourage more branching and root growth.

Maintenance for many groundcovers is minimal, especially if they are evergreen or evergray. If plants are deciduous in winter (e.g. *Erigeron*), cut them back to the crown of the plant before new growth starts. Some groundcovers that are dormant in winter *(Aegopodium)* may simply be covered with a light application of compost before new growth begins.

Deadheading of faded flowers may stimulate new growth and prolonged bloom. *Teucrium cossonii* ssp. *majoricum* is an example of a groundcover that benefits from shearing after the first wave of flowers.

Renewing mulch in a mature groundcover may be difficult. Do this every year when plants are young. Mature plants may not need additional mulch. However, if vigor declines, add a light application of compost in winter.

Achillea ageratifolia

ACHILLEA

Not all the yarrows spread aggressively, overtaking their gentler neighbors. Included here are three species and two hybrid crosses that have been welcome additions to my rock garden, all very well behaved.

Achillea ageratifolia
(Greek yarrow)

A low mat of silver evergray foliage is a focal point in my rock garden in all seasons. This alpine plant is perfectly suited to the lower elevations.

DESCRIPTION

Achillea ageratifolia is under two inches in height, its beautiful silvery-white evergray foliage spreading rapidly, but not aggressively. Leaves are narrow, forming slightly upright rosettes. Because they grow so closely together, the overall effect is a tight mat. White flowers add to the brightness of the plant when it is in bloom in late spring and early summer.

CULTURAL REQUIREMENTS

A native found in the Balkan region, Greek yarrow is definitely cold-tolerant. It is also heat-tolerant.

To maintain the tight growth habit, full sun is the best exposure. If it is used with larger plants growing nearby, they must be kept at a distance so they do not overshadow the Greek yarrow. If this yarrow is shaded at all by adjacent plants at any time during the day, this is likely to cause rotting of foliage, and partial or total die-back.

Greek yarrow must have good drainage. Be especially careful not overwater if it is grown in clay soil. Mature plants in my rock garden have done well with irrigation once every two or three weeks. This is in clay soil that has been amended slightly with compost. The soil is also rocky, which helps with the drainage. Gardeners with sandy soil will be irrigating more frequently, but must watch for signs of overwatering such as yellowing foliage.

A rock mulch is perfect for retaining the surface moisture in the soil while maintaining a dry surface on which the plant may spread.

BLOOM

Open clusters of bright-white flowers may be as small as a half-inch or as wide as one inch, on stems from four to ten inches. Flower clusters are held erect above the foliage. The combination of silver foliage and bright-white bloom is very attractive.

Flowers may be used for cut fresh bouquets or dried for wreaths and everlasting arrangements.

The strongest bloom is in early summer. If the faded flowers are removed, this extends the blooming into midsummer.

SEASONAL INTEREST

Achillea ageratifolia is a very beautiful evergray year-round. In winter especially, when no plants are blooming in my rock garden, the silver of the Greek yarrow adds a strong color dimension.

While the white flowers are very pleasing, it is the tidy and attractive foliage of Greek yarrow that makes it one of my valued rock garden perennials.

COMPANION PLANTS AND LANDSCAPE USE

One of my favorite companions for *Achillea ageratifolia* is *Salvia* 'Berggarten'. The delicate silver-white foliage of the yarrow contrasts beautifully with the green-gray rounded leaves of the sage. And because both are evergray, this contrast may be enjoyed all year!

Any of the other creeping yarrows may be used as companion plants if contrasting foliage is desired. However, because most of them have white blooms they could also be separated by the pink of *Gypsophila repens* 'Rosea' or *Dianthus* species for a stronger contrasting color effect.

Dwarf fescues offer a beautiful textural contrast with Greek yarrow. And the blue tones of the ornamental grasses seem to deepen when grown near the silver-white of the Greek yarrow. Plant the yarrow three feet from the center of the grass. This way the yarrow will not be over-shadowed as both plants mature.

Some of the smaller spring-blooming bulbs such as *Crocus, Galanthus, Scilla,* and *Puschkinia* are lovely spring companions. Small species *Narcissus* are also attractive companions. Do not allow foliage from the bulbs to cover the *Achillea ageratifolia*.

As a small-scale groundcover, Greek yarrow is perfect for dry edges in full sun. Grow it near the edge of a path where its beauty may be enjoyed close-up.

Achillea ageratifolia may also be planted in containers or trough gardens. It will spill over the sides eventually, and do quite well as long as there is sufficient space for its deep root system.

PROPAGATION

Vegetative cuttings may be taken during the growing season. Remove one of the clusters of leaves (a terminal bud) with a short stem section. From the tip of the leaves to the base of the stem you should have about one and one-half inches. Carefully remove the lowest leaves without injuring the stem. Approximately six leaves of varying lengths will remain. See details for propagation in the Introduction.

During the dormant season, divisions may also be carefully removed from the parent plant. Dig into the edges of the plant and find a section that has rooted. If roots are too sparse, some of the foliage may need to be removed.

MAINTENANCE

Deadheading (the removal of faded flowers) will definitely extend the flowering season. Cut back the entire stalk to the crown of the plant. When no stalks are left showing, the plant is more attractive.

This tidy evergray needs very little attention. It is beautiful just as it is!

Achillea Clavennae
(silvery yarrow)

DESCRIPTION

This compact evergray yarrow grows into a tuft of blue-gray foliage. Upon close examination, each small leaf reveals a delicate structure. Clustered along a short stem, the leaves forms rosettes that are attractive when silvery yarrow is not in bloom.

While it has a creeping habit with rhizomes emerging from the central portion of the plant, *Achillea Clavennae* is not an aggressive grower. In comparison to its size aboveground, the root system is quite deep.

A mature plant in my rock garden is twelve inches wide and three inches in height. In early summer, white flowers open on short stems held above the foliage.

CULTURAL REQUIREMENTS

This alpine treasure is endemic to the central and eastern Alps, growing at an elevation as high as 8000 feet and as low as 4000 feet. Fortunately, for those of us who garden at even lower elevations, *Achillea Clavennae* adjusts to the vagaries of our climates and their dissimilarities from the high elevations where it grows natively.

Form is most attractive when the plant is grown in full sun. The bright summer sunlight in the foothills is perfect. Grown closer to the coast where fog is a factor, or in partial shade, silvery yarrow will be more open in its growth habit.

Achillea Clavennae does not grow well in rich soil. To my rocky clay soil, I have added 20% compost and a generous amount of colloidal phosphate to encourage good root growth. The addition of oyster shell in my acidic soil is important for this plant. Natively it grows in soil of a higher pH.

In my rock garden, silvery yarrow is growing in full sun on a sloped south face. Deep irrigation once every three weeks in the heat of the summer has been adequate for a mature plant. In areas with no summer rains, silvery yarrow will suffer without irrigation.

The best mulch is a small gravel, which prevents lower leaves from rotting.

BLOOM

Ivory-white flowers are small open discs, less than a quarter of an inch wide, clustered at the end of the five to eight-inch stems. While in the higher mountains this perennial will bloom for a few months, in my Sierra foothill garden, *Achillea Clavennae* blooms heavily in May and June, then sporadically until fall.

Though stems are short, sprays of silvery yarrow are quite nice in miniature bouquets. As dried flowers they're not notable, perhaps because I am comparing them to the outstanding form and color of the larger *Achillea tomentosa* 'Maynard's Gold'.

SEASONAL INTEREST

The blue-gray foliage of *Achillea Clavennae* is the same hue in all seasons in my garden. An uncommon color, this compact evergray is attractive all year. In early summer, the white flowers are a pleasing contrast to both its own foliage and its colorful neighboring plants.

COMPANION PLANTS AND LANDSCAPE USE

Silvery yarrow is attractive grown near the fescues or other small sun-loving grasses. May and June-blooming rock garden perennials (*Thymus, Dianthus, Phlox*) join in the colorful display in early summer, their vibrant flowers perfect companions to the white yarrow blossoms. However, I do not plant *Achillea Clavennae* near the glistening white of snow-in-summer (*Cerastium*). The blooms of silvery yarrow are dull white in comparison!

Because *Achillea Clavennae* is not a strong spreader it serves as a groundcover only on a small-scale. This makes it an excellent choice for a rock garden or alpine container garden. No need worry about this one taking over the neighboring plants! In fact, do not allow companion plants to overshadow or shade this compact alpine. Used as an edging plant, keep silvery yarrow in full sun, away from plants that might cast shadows.

PROPAGATION

Achillea Clavennae is easily propagated from vegetative cuttings taken March through October. Misting will hasten root development, but do not keep the young plant growing in moist conditions for too long. When roots have formed, move the rooted cutting into a small container of potting soil with perlite for good drainage.

Depending on growing conditions, slowly spreading rhizomes may form shoots that will root in place and provide new plants when removed from the parent. Check for these tiny roots to ensure that you have a good plant start, pot it as you would your rooted cutting, then give it a few weeks to grow under your watchful eye before placing it in the garden.

Seeds are very fine and must be sown on the surface of a loose planting medium. Allow seeds to mature before removing the flower stem from the parent plant. Seeds are ready when a spent flower cluster shaken over your hand or a piece of paper reveals hundreds of seeds. If you are seed-saving, only one cluster will supply you with plenty of seed.

Divisions of *Achillea Clavennae* may also be made to increase your planting or share with friends. With a mature plant these divisions may be removed without disturbing the primary root. Though this may be done at any time of the year, if the divisions are not well-rooted they will need to be treated as young or slightly rooted cuttings. A division with lots of roots taken during the dormant season in late fall or winter may be planted directly into the garden.

MAINTENANCE

VERY EASY! This perfect little evergray yarrow needs little attention. Spent flowers may be removed, cutting the stalk all the way back inside the mound of foliage so that it doesn't show as a dead stick. In fact, deadheading as soon as the flowers fade will encourage more blooms during the summer months.

Achillea tomentosa 'Maynard's Gold'

Achillea millefolium
(common yarrow)

This groundcover is an excellent substitute for lawn. It is also excellent as an edging plant, especially along a dry edge of a flower border or driveway. *Achillea millefolium* may be overshadowed by nearby taller perennials or shrubs, and will also thrive in full hot sun. For details, refer to "Deer in My Garden, Vol. 1".

Achillea tomentosa
(woolly yarrow)

In my rock garden are two woolly yarrows with distinctly different growth habits. One is a strong, though not aggressive, spreader and one species is diminutive and compact.

Achillea tomentosa 'Maynard's Gold'
('Maynard's Gold' woolly yarrow)

This perennial groundcover highlights the late spring rock garden with its glowing flower color. Vigorous when it is not overshadowed by neighboring plants, this spreading groundcover is one of the most attractive of evergrays in my rock garden.

DESCRIPTION

'Maynard's Gold' woolly yarrow hugs the ground with soft, felty gray-white leaves, creeping along the ground in rosettes. If there is a rock in the way, it climbs right over it, or around it! While it is not an aggressive yarrow, this strong perennial can spread to three feet from a single four-inch container within a few years. Its height is under two to three inches (this depends upon the fertility of the soil and irrigation practices).

In late spring, strong six to ten-inch stems hold umbels of gold flowers to three inches across the flowerheads.

CULTURAL REQUIREMENTS

Similar to the other creeping yarrows, woolly yarrow grows in the coldest regions of the western United States and is very heat-tolerant.

Achillea tomentosa 'Maynard's Gold' is a strong perennial, but particular about its likes and dislikes. Full sun is a definite requirement year-round. Whether planted in the rock garden or used as a large-scale groundcover, this creeper needs soil with good drainage, especially in winter.

Do not allow winter shadows from rocks. Keep this yarrow on the sunny side. It's perfect for a south or west-facing slope.

While woolly yarrow will spread over rocky soils, it must root as it creeps in some soil. The best form is when it is grown in soil that is not too rich. In my garden, I have added approximately 25% organic compost to my native clay soil, plus oyster shell and rock phosphate as discussed in the Introduction.

Gray foliage often indicates a plant that is xeriphitic. However, this yarrow did not perform well on a dry edge of my rock garden. A good soaking every two to three weeks in the heat of the summer now keeps it thriving.

BLOOM

Golden clusters of flowers brighten the early summer garden. The size of these heads depends on the fertility of the soil. In my gravelly rock garden that is basically clay soil plus compost, each cluster is about two inches across. *Achillea tomentosa* 'Maynard's Gold' has very strong stems six to ten inches in length, making them perfect for cutting.

With deadheading, bloom may extend to four to six weeks.

The color holds nicely when new blossoms are picked to dry for winter bouquets. Fading flowers will not have the strength of color when they dry. This also an excellent everlasting for fall or winter wreaths. Weave it into a grape vine base with a few dry ornamental grasses for a perfect and simple fall decoration.

SEASONAL INTEREST

Because it is evergray, this perennial adds strength and interest to the border year-round. While the display of gold flowers is dynamic, it is the soft rosettes of gray foliage that offer the longest season of attractive color.

COMPANION PLANTS AND LANDSCAPE USE

Achillea tomentosa 'Maynard's Gold' may certainly be used as an edging plant as long as it is not overshadowed by adjacent plants. This creeping plant wants its own space! Equally important is that it have good drainage and not be overwatered. Companion plants nearby would need to be low-irrigation such as *Penstemon hirsutus*, *Erigeron karvinskianus* (Santa Barbara daisy), *Lavandula angustifolia nana* 'Alba' (dwarf white lavender), *Dianthus* species (pink), or another creeping yarrow.

I prefer to grow this yarrow in my rock garden, which is watered every two to three weeks in the heat of the summer. It's placed in as sunny as possible an exposure with no aggressive plants growing nearby.

In a container, plant this yarrow in a loose mix with perlite added to ensure drainage. Do not overwater.

PROPAGATION

It is possible to take vegetative cuttings of *Achillea tomentosa* 'Maynard's Gold' during the growing season. They sometimes rot in humid conditions before they root, so the rooting medium must have at least one-half perlite or more to one-half vermiculite. Check the cuttings frequently, and move them to drier conditions as soon as they have begun to root.

In late fall, winter, or very early spring, the edges of your primary plant may have rosettes with roots. These may easily be transplanted, cutting them from the parent plant with little disturbance.

While I have not propagated this plant from seed, I have had volunteers in my nursery, which tells me that it's probably fairly easy. The seed is quite fine and should be sown on the soil surface.

MAINTENANCE

I usually cut the faded flower stalks to the base. This encourages a little more bloom, and certainly makes this beautiful plant look very tidy in my rock garden.

Achillea tomentosa 'Moonlight'
('Moonlight' woolly yarrow)

This tiny evergreen is one of my favorite rock garden perennials. Perhaps this is because I must be so attentive to it, to ensure that it is not overshadowed by more aggressive rock garden treasures.

DESCRIPTION

'Moonlight' yarrow has soft blue-green leaves with a lacy structure. The overall effect of this evergreen plant is a very tight mound, but on close examination, the clusters of leaves in rosettes indicates its similarity to *Achillea* 'Maynard's Gold'.

In my garden, *Achillea tomentosa* 'Moonlight' has never grown larger than five inches in width with a height under one inch, making it one of the smallest plants in my rock garden. Small clusters of pale-yellow flowers appear on short stems in early summer.

CULTURAL REQUIREMENTS

Full sun is the best exposure for this yarrow to optimize bloom, but light afternoon shade will not affect the growth. Easily overshadowed by neighboring plants, keep this treasure growing where there is no competition. In my rock garden a volunteer appeared within an open area of *Antennaria,* and is doing quite well.

While good drainage is essential, 'Moonlight' yarrow will not survive unless it is watered every two to three weeks in clay soil. Gardeners with sandy soil will need to water more often.

Mulch with small gravel or rocks.

BLOOM

Clusters of very tiny flowers in flat heads open a bright pale-yellow in early summer. The brightness soon fades, but the flower clusters remain a pale-yellow for a few weeks.

Flower stems are three to four inches in height. Because they are so short, cut flowers may be used only for the tiniest of fresh or dried arrangements.

SEASONAL INTEREST

A diminutive evergreen, *Achillea tomentosa* 'Moonlight' needs to be grown where you will pause to enjoy it year around. My best specimen is growing near the gravel walk to my vegetable garden gate. And it is opposite a bench I frequent. While it is a volunteer, it couldn't be better placed for my appreciation.

COMPANION PLANTS AND LANDSCAPE USE

The 'Moonlight' yarrow in my garden found its favorite companion: *Antennaria dioica* (pussy toes). I have added small *Galanthus* bulbs for a spring focal point.

Erinus alpinus (alpine liver-balsam) is also a good companion plant with contrasting foliage and flower color, and similar size. Its purple flowers are a pleasing contrast to the pale-yellow of *Achillea tomentosa* 'Moonlight'.

Other companions for *Achillea tomentosa* 'Moonlight' include *Saponaria pumilio* (soapwort), and *Erysimum helveticum* (alpine wall-flower).

The tiniest and tightest of the thymes, *Thymus serpyllum minus* may be grown nearby as a companion. Its flat appearance will make the 'Moonlight' yarrow appear more mounded.

Use this little yarrow for the niches in rock walls where it may have its own space and grow to its full beauty. The wall must be facing south to expose the yarrow to as full sun as possible. Remember that in niches, the rocks will cast some shadows.

In small alpine containers, 'Moonlight' yarrow gains strength in scale.

While it may be the smallest plant in a larger rock garden, its size is to an advantage in a planter. It does not need a lot of space for its root system or for the above-ground plant.

PROPAGATION

Working close to the crown, cut off rooted divisions and treat them as vegetative cuttings. They will need high humidity for a couple of weeks, and no direct exposure to the sun. Bright light under 40% shade cloth has worked well for my attempts to increase my stock. Watch carefully for signs of growth which will indicate increased rooting. Move the plants to brighter light and decrease the humidity.

Seeing a volunteer in the perfect spot in my rock garden has taught me that growing more *Achillea tomentosa* 'Moonlight' from seed should be easy. The seed is very fine and should not be covered, but should be sown on top of a very loose medium.

MAINTENANCE

Easy! Even if faded flowers are not removed, the small stalks seem to wither and disappear into the plant. Removing the stalks as flowers fade will keep the plant looking its tidiest. If you are seed-saving, wait until the seeds are mature. Hold the heads steady so that the seed will not scatter, and cut the stalk back at the crown of the plant.

Achillea x kellereri

I have been unable to find a common name for this rare evergray yarrow. Many years ago I obtained it through my membership in the American Rock Garden Society. This yarrow is cited in "Index Hortensis, Vol. 1: Perennials" as a cross of *A. ageratifolia* ssp. *aizoon* and *A. clypeolata*. It would be interesting to introduce *A. clypeolata* into my garden to study its characteristics, and to see whether the deer would include it in their diet.

DESCRIPTION

Achillea x *kellereri*

Achillea x *kellereri* is a beautiful evergray rock garden plant, with similarities to other yarrows I have written about in leaf form and flowering habit. However, it is quite different in overall appearance.

Very long and narrow gray leaves to four inches give the plant a fine texture and mounding form. With a slight bluish cast, the toothed leaves are almost as silver-white as *Achillea ageratifolia.*

Achillea x *kellereri* spreads slowly as a mounding plant. My mature plant is almost fifteen inches in width.

White flowers begin to open in late May and continue through June in my rock garden.

CULTURAL REQUIREMENTS

Achillea x *kellereri* has survived winter cold with no snow cover to 8°F in my garden. Because of its genetic lineage, I would expect it to survive much colder temperatures. Remember that most of these rock garden yarrows originate in the Alps and Balkans.

Full sun is required to keep the plant from getting leggy. It even thrives with reflected heat from nearby rocks, and hot summer temperatures.

Silver and gray yarrows like good drainage, and this yarrow is no exception. The lower leaves will yellow if it has been watered too much. Try irrigating every two to three weeks with clay soil, and every ten to fourteen days with sandy soils.

BLOOM

Sturdy stalks six to ten inches in height hold clusters of white flowers one inch wide. The white is bright and attractive.

Bloom begins in late May and continues through June. A few more blooms continue sporadically through the summer if deadheading has been done on a regular basis.

Because of the long stems, this is a good flower for cut arrangements even if the flowerheads are not large. It may also be dried as an everlasting.

SEASONAL INTEREST

This yarrow is evergray and quite interesting in the winter garden. The foliage and form make it a focal plant year-round.

COMPANION PLANTS AND LANDSCAPE USE

Combine *Achillea* x *kellereri* with perennials of similar height and spread, and do not grow it near aggressive plants. One of my favorite combinations is with the yellow or scarlet *Penstemon pinifolius*. Either color or both will benefit from the contrasting white of the yarrow.

Erinus alpinus is also a nice companion. Its dark-green mounding habit makes the silvery-white yarrow look lacy and delicate. The purple flowers of the *Erinus* bloom at the same time as the white yarrow, a pleasing contrast.

I have used *Allium moly* nearby, being careful not to plant the bulbs too close to the yarrow. Its cheerful yellow flowers open when the yarrow is blooming.

Placing beautiful rocks into the soil (one-fourth buried, three-fourths above ground) near the yarrow heightens its value as a landscape plant. The finely-toothed leaves are even more attractive when played against a rock.

PROPAGATION

Vegetative cuttings may be taken during the growing season. With a sharp knife or scissors, remove about half of each leaf to reduce length. If a portion is not removed, the leaves may continue to wilt, delaying rooting.

I have a few volunteers in my rock garden. Because this plant does not supply a lot of cutting material, sowing the fine seed on top of the soil may be the best way to increase the numbers. Do not cover the seed.

MAINTENANCE

This plant is attractive in or out of bloom, but deadheading will ensure a continuing bloom into midsummer.

Occasionally with spring cleanup, a few of the lower leaves may need to be removed if they have died during the winter.

Achillea x 'King Edward'
('King Edward' creeping yarrow)

This lovely, compact evergray yarrow differs from other cultivars in the genus in growth habit, flower and foliage color. It is a hybrid, a cross of *Achillea tomentosa* and *A. argentea.* In the nursery trade it may be labeled as an *Achillea tomentosa.*

DESCRIPTION

Very narrow, gray-green leaves form open evergray rosettes, giving the plant a slight mounding appearance to a height of three to four inches. Pale-yellow flowers bloom above foliage. While it is spreading, a mature plant may reach only eighteen inches in width.

CULTURAL REQUIREMENTS

Achillea x 'King Edward' is another evergray yarrow that will grow in the coldest regions of the western United States. Similar to other xeriphitic plants with gray, silver, or even white foliage, 'King Edward' thrives in the summer heat of the Sierra Nevada foothills.

Somewhat more tolerant of irrigation than other gray or silver yarrows, this one still likes to be on the dry side with the irrigation every two weeks or less in clay soil. Gardeners with sandy soil will be irrigating more frequently.

Keep this yarrow in full sun, but away from dry edges.

BLOOM

Pale-yellow flowers in open clusters form on very strong stems to six inches in height in early summer. Blooming lasts for several weeks. When deadheaded, bloom continues through most of August.

The flower stalks have alternating leaves, echoing the form of the primary foliage, but much smaller. These exquisitely fringed leaves are perfect for pressing.

'King Edward' yarrow is delightful for a bouquet of small cut flowers, its color and form holding for several days if it is picked when flowers have first opened.

SEASONAL INTEREST

As an evergray, *Achillea* x 'King Edward' adds year-round interest to the rock garden or border.

In late spring and early summer the pale-yellow flowers held above the gray-green foliage add a soft color contrast.

COMPANION PLANTS AND LANDSCAPE USE

Place 'King Edward' yarrow near the bright pinks of *Dianthus gratianopolitanus* (cheddar pink) for a pleasing contrast. Even the pale-pink *Dianthus erinaceus* is a good companion to this yarrow.

The whites of other yarrows and of *Erigeron karvinskianus* (Santa Barbara daisy) are also soft contrasts to the blossoms of *Achillea* x 'King Edward'.

I think this plant is lost in a larger border, and prefer to use it in my rock garden. However, I could see its use at the edge of sunny steps, spilling onto the pathway without consuming too much space.

As a container plant, 'King Edward' yarrow does quite well. Use it as a single specimen or combined with other compact rock garden treasures. Do not grow it adjacent to larger plants that might overshadow its foliage and form.

PROPAGATION

To propagate *Achillea* x 'King Edward', take vegetative cuttings during the most active growing season (May through August) but do not allow them to stay in humid conditions once roots begin to form. A mature plant may also provide additional planting material from the edges of the parent plant. In late fall, dig carefully into the edges of the plant and look for rooted portions that may be removed and transplanted.

Because this perennial is a cross, seed may not give you progeny true to its parent.

MAINTENANCE

Deadheading faded blooms by cutting the flower stalk back to the base will encourage more flowering, stronger spreading, and also make the plant more attractive for the remainder of the growing season and into winter.

Aegopodium podagraria 'Variegata'

AEGOPODIUM

Aegopodium podagraria 'Variegata'
(bishop's weed, goutweed)

A beautiful variegated groundcover for semi-shade, bishop's weed is dormant in winter, but reappears very early in spring with its lush growth of attractive foliage.

DESCRIPTION

An aggressively growing groundcover, *Aegopodium podagraria* is not for the small garden or for the edge of a perennial border. In fact, even in larger areas, gardeners may want to control its rampant habit with physical barriers.

Height of plant depends on how rich the soil is and how much irrigation water the plant receives. I have one stand that is about eight inches in height, but I have seen it in some gardens where it is as tall as one foot.

My garden is large enough that I can allow it to grow where wanted by summer irrigation. Bishop's weed doesn't like roots dry, so it stops growing when it spreads into dry areas. Of course this system of control will not work where gardeners have summer rains or even fog!

The attractive light-green and white leaves grow densely. Delicate sprays of creamy-white flowers are held above the foliage in early summer.

CULTURAL REQUIREMENTS

Aegopodium podagraria grows in the coldest mountain and intermountain regions in the western United States.

Full sun to light shade are good exposures in areas that have summer clouds or fog. In my hot area of the Sierra Nevada foothills, with unrelenting sun in the summer, bishop's weed prefers partial or even full shade. Afternoon shade or dappled sunlight all day will work well.

Perennial bishop's weed loves rich soil with lots of compost. The richer the soil, the lusher the foliage.

Regular irrigation is necessary. In my clay loam, *Aegopodium podagraria* volunteers and spreads under my nursery benches where it is happy with the daily irrigation in the heat of the summer. In the main garden I'm not willing to water that much. With once a week irrigation and partial shade, bishop's weed still makes a pretty groundcover. It's just not as lush.

A good thick mulch of organic material will provide nutrients and reduce water requirements. Shredded bark, compost, leaves, or decomposed straw are excellent choices. Or use a combination of any of these materials, renewing the mulch when *Aegopodium podagraria* is dormant in winter.

BLOOM

Tiny white flowers bloom in open sprays in early summer.

Flowers are not significant, but the delicate sprays add a textural interest in a small garden or container.

SEASONAL INTEREST

Bishop's weed is dormant in winter. However, its growth season is quite long since it emerges in early spring and does not disappear until winter temperatures have signaled an end to growth.

COMPANION PLANTS AND LANDSCAPE USE

Because of its aggressive growing habit, the best companion plants for bishop's weed are shrubs and trees. A groundcover of *Aegopodium podagraria* may be established under a deep-rooted tree such as a dogwood (*Cornus florida*) or linden (*Tilia cordata*).

This is an effective groundcover under *Choisya ternata* (Mexican orange) and *Lonicera nitida* (box honeysuckle).

Shallow-rooted shrubs and trees may have too much root competition for bishop's weed to thrive in their zone. However, if good soil preparation is done initially and compost is added as a mulch each winter, this difficulty of competition for nutrients may be overcome.

Bishop's weed may easily be grown in a container, but will be dormant in winter.

Do not grow bishop's weed close to other perennials or groundcovers. It is far too aggressive.

PROPAGATION

Aegopodium podagraria may be divided at any time of the year. I prefer to do this during the dormant season since the leaves wilt so easily when the plant is lifted. Even a young plant will provide many divisions.

MAINTENANCE

EASY! Faded blooms seem to fade into the foliage. And when the foliage itself wanes after a few frosts in early winter, just spread compost to renew the mulch and add nutrients to the soil.

Ajuga 'Caitlin's Giant'

AJUGA

Ajuga reptans
(carpet bugle)

This common evergreen groundcover is the species that spreads by runners and includes several cultivars. The ones included here have been grown in my garden and left alone by the deer. The genus *Ajuga* also includes rock garden species that do not spread by runners. These may also be deer-resistant, but I have not grown them.

DESCRIPTION

Ajuga 'Caitlin's Giant' is the largest *Ajuga* I have grown. The outer dark-green leaves of each rosette may be as long as eight inches. Each rosette is eight to ten inches in width. Flowers are dark-blue.

Ajuga 'Burgundy Lace' (*Ajuga* 'Tricolor') is smaller and more compact. Variegated foliage with white, pink, and reddish-purple is very attractive. Larger leaves are under five inches in length. The shorter leaves and each rosette give an overall flatter appearance to the groundcover.

Flowers are periwinkle-blue. In very cold winter temperatures, partial die-back is not unusual.

Ajuga 'Chocolate Chip' is the most compact *Ajuga* I have grown. While it does spread by runners, its two to three-inch leaves give the rosettes a tighter appearance than 'Caitlin's Giant'. This evergreen groundcover is an attractive accent in a small space.

CULTURAL REQUIREMENTS

Ajuga has a very broad range of cold and heat tolerance. As noted, partial die-back in very cold winter temperatures is not unusual, but in most areas, *Ajuga* is evergreen.

Full to partial sun is the best exposure. The deeper the color of the leaves, the more sun the plant will tolerate. The cultivar 'Burgundy Lace' may need some shade in areas that have particularly hot and sunny summers. However, planted in too much shade *Ajuga* 'Burgundy Lace' will not have the rich variation of colors.

This evergreen perennial groundcover likes lots of water. While I am able to grow it in my garden with summer irrigation once a week in clay soil, carpet bugle grows much better in my nursery where irrigation may be as frequent as daily.

Soil preparation does not need to be deep but must be rich with lots of compost and rock powders. Preparation to one foot is more than adequate, and even six inches will work as long as the soil is very high in humus.

Because this plant makes such a tight groundcover, and because it is evergreen, adding mulches should be done with the initial planting.

BLOOM

Bloom begins in late spring, and continues into the summer.

Blue flowers are quite attractive, blooming in clusters along sturdy stalks. The flowering stalks of the cultivar 'Caitlin's Giant' may be as tall as ten to twelve inches when the plant is growing in optimal conditions. This *Ajuga* has very beautiful dark-blue flowers that are wonderful cut flowers.

Stalks of 'Burgundy Lace' are usually under six inches with periwinkle-blue flowers. 'Chocolate Chip' stalks are even shorter with mid-blue flowers. Both cultivars may be used for miniature arrangements.

SEASONAL INTEREST

Ajuga species look great year-round. Whether it is used in small areas as an accent, or larger areas as a groundcover, *Ajuga* is a strong foliage plant.

COMPANION PLANTS AND LANDSCAPE USE

Ajuga reptans is an aggressive and tight evergreen groundcover that leaves room for nothing else. However, it may be used as an edging in combination with other plants as long as its appetite for space is curbed. Decide how much space you will allow it in your garden, and place a barrier to keep it from invading other plants.

I frequently grow bulbs in containers. In spring, when they are looking their most beautiful, I place a container in the middle of the *Ajuga* if the combination pleases me. This year it was a full container of *Narcissus* 'Little Gem', an early-blooming miniature daffodil, nestled into the dark-green leaves of 'Caitlin's Giant'. When the bulbs fade, the container is removed. While the groundcover will be damaged under the container, it quickly recovers.

The same method could be used for a pot of summer color. In deer country, annual lobelia, alyssum, vinca and sometimes even dwarf zinnia may not be damaged.

Use any of the carpet bugle as container plants. With this method of growing these beautiful evergreens, you can optimize the nutrients with a good container mix, concentrate your watering in a smaller area, and discipline the growth.

PROPAGATION

Since *Ajuga reptans* grows quickly by runners, small rosettes may be removed as soon as they have rooted. For larger plants, dig up sections of the groundcover and divide or plant as an entire clump.

Ajuga may also be propagated from cuttings taken during the growing season.

MAINTENANCE

EASY! No maintenance is required, unless you want to remove faded flowers stalks back to the base. I never seem to get to this task, and they just magically disappear, collapsing into the foliage.

Alchemilla mollis

Alchemilla mollis
(lady's mantle)

Alchemilla mollis is a beautiful perennial for a groundcover in partial shade, an edging plant, or as a single specimen in an irrigated rock garden in afternoon shade. Refer to "Deer in My Garden, Vol. 1" for detailed information.

Alyssum montanum

ALYSSUM

The genus *Alyssum* includes two evergray trailing species which the deer have left alone in my rock garden, *Alyssum montanum* and *Alyssum tortuosum*. I have tried the more common *Alyssum saxitile* (*Aurinia saxatilis*) 'Flore Pleno', but the deer have always eaten its soft gray leaves. Smaller, but similar in appearance, though the leaves are not as soft, is *Alyssum petraeum* 'Compactum' (*A. saxatile* 'Compactum') which does not seem to interest the deer in my garden.

Alyssum montanum 'Mountain Gold' (*A. montanum* 'Berggold')
(mountain alyssum)

The fragrant flowers and attractive foliage of *Alyssum montanum* make this evergray perennial worthy of including in any rock garden.

DESCRIPTION

'Mountain Gold' alyssum has a deep root and spreads primarily from the central crown, to a very refined two feet. This wonderful perennial is definitely not aggressive. Trailing stems cover each other, and height is rarely more than eight inches.

Small leaves (about one-half inch in length) are light gray-green on gray stems. The overall effect of the plant is gray.

Fragrant bright-yellow flowers are held above the foliage, opening in late spring and early summer.

CULTURAL REQUIREMENTS

Alyssum montanum grows in the coldest zones of the western United States, with or without a snow cover.

Full sun is the required exposure to keep the plant compact. Leggy plants are not as attractive and will not bloom as much.

Soil should not be too rich, but the addition of some compost and rock powders will ensure healthy, long-lived plants. Add oyster shell in acidic soils to release nutrients.

A deep irrigation once every two to three weeks in the heat of the summer has worked well for *Alyssum* grown in my clay and rocky soil. *Alyssum* watered too frequently will develop yellowing of lower leaves. Those leaves will eventually fall off, and plants may need to be cut back to encourage new growth.

A gravelly or rocky mulch is ideal for conserving surface moisture, preventing compaction from rains, and keeping the stems and foliage as dry as possible.

BLOOM

'Mountain Gold' alyssum's clusters of flowers are bright-yellow and fragrant, opening in early summer. Gardeners near coastal areas and in more mild climates may enjoy these pretty flowers in late spring. The appearance of the flowers is similar to the blossoms of annual sweet alyssum (*Lobularia maritima*).

Flowering lasts a few weeks, and may be extended if the first blossoms to open are removed as soon as they fade.

SEASONAL INTEREST

Alyssum montanum is evergray, but the loose growth of its branching stems does not make it an outstanding plant for the winter garden. However, it is not dormant so it might be of interest trailing over a wall.

COMPANION PLANTS AND LANDSCAPE USE

Because it is not aggressive in growth habit, *Alyssum montanum* is a good companion with many other rock garden plants. Its bright-yellow flowers are pleasing with the whites of creeping yarrow. In contrast to the very silvery foliage of some yarrows, mountain alyssum has a blue cast to its gray leaves.

Paired with *Aethionema* 'Warley Rose' in the rock garden or in a container, the two evergreen perennials become a focal point with their early color, and provide up-close interest year-round.

A rock wall facing south is another planting opportunity for perennial alyssum. Planted above the wall, it trails over beautifully without obscuring the rocks. Planting 'Mountain Gold' within the wall as it is built is also a nice effect. In this setting use *Aubrieta deltoidea* as a companion. The purple and gold flowers should open at the same time in most garden climates for a dynamic color combination.

PROPAGATION

Vegetative cuttings of *Alyssum montanum* root very quickly. As with most gray-leafed plants, it is important to plant them as soon as possible after rooting, and move them to an area of lower humidity (see Introduction).

Do not attempt to divide *Alyssum montanum*, as this may injure the primary root system.

MAINTENANCE

EASY! Deadheading faded flowers by removing only the portion that has bloomed will encourage more flowering.

Antennaria dioica 'Rosea'

Antennaria dioica 'Rosea'
(pussy toes, cat's-foot)

Antennaria dioica is the only species I have grown. It is a common species in the European mountains, found in elevations to 9800 feet, and appearing in lower elevations below 2000-foot elevation. Pussy toes has also naturalized in North America.

DESCRIPTION

Antennaria dioica has beautiful silver-gray foliage with a blue cast. The underside of the leaf is silver-white. Foliage is slightly woolly and clusters in attractive rosettes, with tiny leaves in the center and leaves to one-inch length at the base of the rosette. The size of each rosette varies considerably.

Antennaria spreads slowly on short stolons, forming an evergray mat close to the ground. Height of foliage is under two inches and spread is three feet or more. Height in bloom is three to four inches.

CULTURAL REQUIREMENTS

Antennaria dioica tolerates very cold temperatures throughout North America.

Grow pussy toes in full sun or light shade, as long as drainage is excellent in all seasons. When I first planted *Antennaria dioica* in partial shade in clay soil, it spread out of the rocky clay soil and into the loose small gravel in the nearby path, where it grew much better.

I now have a strong plant at the top of a mound of rocky clay soil in full sun. Soil preparation should be minimal, but compost and organic phosphorus need to be added in clay or sandy soils. Gardeners with acidic soil should also add oyster shell.

Irrigation once every two weeks is ideal if *Antennaria dioica* has good drainage. It definitely tolerates less frequent watering.

Mulches should be small rocks or gravel.

BLOOM

Look closely at the flowers. *Antennaria dioica* is in the *Asteraceae* family, related to daisies. Each cluster of flowers on three-inch stalks begins as a tight button of buds, expanding to miniature pink daisies, and finishing as a fluffy head. Bloom lasts for several weeks, in late spring and early summer.

Deadheading is not necessary. Faded flowers and stalks will soon disappear.

SEASONAL INTEREST

Antennaria dioica is a beautiful evergray for year-round interest. When it is grown in good drainage, it is as attractive in winter as it is at the height of the growing season.

Flowers are interesting, but not highly colorful. It is the foliage of this plant that adds strength to the garden.

COMPANION PLANTS AND LANDSCAPE USE

Antennaria dioica must not be overshadowed by larger or more aggressive plants. It is a beautiful evergray small-scale groundcover.

Good companions include smaller alpines: *Erysimum helveticum* (alpine wallflower), *Erinus alpinus* (alpine liver-balsam), *Achillea tomentosa* 'Moonlight' (dwarf woolly yarrow), and *Thymus serpyllum minus*.

Grown on the sunny side of rocks, either above or in a wall, or within stepping stones, *Antennaria dioica* is a valuable landscape plant in dry areas.

When using this low-irrigation perennial groundcover edging a walkway or within stepping stones, irrigation may be only when you wash the walk with water.

Antennaria dioica is a tough plant that will thrive in southern and western exposures in full sun, even on a slope.

The dry semi-shade on the south side of a native oak is one landscape situation where *Antennaria dioica* is effective. In autumn, if the oak is deciduous, leaves must be removed when they fall.

PROPAGATION

Vegetative cuttings taken as large or small rosettes during the growing season root easily. They should be planted as soon as they have rooted, and moved to drier conditions.

Divisions may also be made in late fall or early spring by removing a portion of the plant that has rooted as it spreads. *Antennaria dioica* is touchy about division, so do not attempt this during winter cold spells.

MAINTENANCE

VERY, VERY EASY! No maintenance is necessary. Fussy gardeners may use their tiny scissors to cut back faded flower stalks.

Arabis caucasica

ARABIS

Arabis species are attractive evergreens for the rock garden or as ground-covers in small areas. Included here are four species grown in my garden. Because the deer have never done any damage, I would predict that all species with this genus would be good choices in deer country.

Arabis caucasica (A. albida)
(wall rockcress)

This rockcress is a native from the Mediterranean region. It is one of the earliest plants to bloom in my garden, its fragrant flowers inviting me to linger in the garden in spring.

DESCRIPTION

Arabis caucasica spreads to form an evergray mat a foot and a half wide.

Two to three-inch gray-green leaves grow densely, giving the plant a height just under six inches. Fragrant white flowers bloom in profusion.

The root system of rockcress is quite fine, with multiple absorbing roots rather than the taproot typical of so many rock garden plants.

The cultivar 'Variegata' has gray-green leaves edged with creamy white.

CULTURAL REQUIREMENTS

Arabis caucasica will grow in the coldest regions of the western United States.

Gardeners near the coast and those who have some cloud cover during the summer may grow this plant in full sun. In my hot-summer region in the Sierra foothills, *Arabis caucasica* does best with afternoon shade. However, it must not be in full shade in winter. Finding the perfect place for this plant takes awareness of its cultural requirements, and attention to the changes in available light from season to season.

In the rock garden, plant this *Arabis* where a large rock will provide a cool area for the root in the afternoon if the garden is in full sun. Planting on a mound, plant on the east side.

The cultivar 'Variegata' must have bright shade or dappled sunlight all day.

Soil should be amended with compost and rock powders, but should not be too rich. Good drainage is essential, especially in winter. If your soil is rocky or gravelly, this plant will be quite happy with a little compost, phosphorus and oyster shell added. No need to remove those rocks!

Arabis caucasica needs to be irrigated on a regular basis. In clay soil, two weeks between irrigations in summer heat may not be often enough. Rockcress has grown better where I irrigated it once a week or every ten days. Overwatering will cause lower leaves to yellow.

A mulch may be organic as long as stems are not covered. Too much moisture under the plant may cause rotting of leaves. Gravel and small rocks are also good mulches.

BLOOM

The very delicate flowers of rockcress are bright-white and very fragrant. They bloom so abundantly that the foliage is almost covered. Flowers have four petals and are just under half an inch.

Flowers bloom on very delicate stems making them difficult to use as cut flowers. They also wilt easily. Enjoy this one in the garden where the bloom lasts for three to four weeks in spring.

SEASONAL INTEREST

As long as it has strong light and good drainage in winter, this evergray perennial looks wonderful in the garden year-round. It is particularly attractive in late spring when it is almost covered with white flowers.

COMPANION PLANTS AND LANDSCAPE USE

Allowing for its spreading habit, *Arabis caucasica* may be grown as an edging plant near taller perennials as long as they do not overshadow the rockcress. *Penstemon hirsutus* and *P. pinifolius* may be grown three feet from the rockcress (center to center). As mature plants they will meet.

Arabis caucasica is also excellent as a specimen plant in a rock garden. Its relatively small size (eighteen-inch to two-foot spread) and nonaggressive growth habit make it an appealing choice for an accent.

Several plants of rockcress spaced twelve to fifteen inches apart create an attractive groundcover.

Arabis caucasica 'Variegata' has similar usage in partial shade. Companion plants must include perennials that will tolerate a similar exposure, such as *Alchemilla mollis* (lady's mantle), *Helleborus* (hellebore), and *Iris unguicularis* (winter iris).

Both forms of *Arabis caucasica* are excellent in containers.

Note: while I have not grown the pink cultivars of *Arabis caucasica*, 'Rosa-Bella' and 'Pink Charm', I would expect them to be deer-resistant.

PROPAGATION

Arabis caucasica may be rooted from vegetative cuttings taken during the growing season. Watch for signs of rooting and plant the cuttings into compost with perlite as soon as possible.

MAINTENANCE

EASY! A very undemanding evergray, *Arabis caucasica* needs little attention. Removal of the faded flowers stalks is not necessary, but may add to the attractiveness of the plant in early summer. Eventually the flower stalks will fall into the foliage.

Arabis Ferdinandi-Coburgi 'Variegata'
(variegated rockcress)

I purchased my original plant labeled as *Arabis Fernando-Coburgi*. I have since noted that "Hortus Third" indentifies it as *A. Ferdinandi-Coburgi*, and "Index Hortensis" as *A. ferdinandi-coburgii*.

This beautiful small rockcress is an evergreen treasure native to Bulgaria.

DESCRIPTION

Small green and white leaves, the longest about an inch in length, form compact evergreen rosettes under three inches in height. *Arabis Ferdinandi-Coburgi* 'Variegata' spreads to about one foot. Very delicate white flowers are lightly scented.

CULTURAL REQUIREMENTS

Arabis Ferdinandi-Coburgi 'Variegata' will not tolerate the coldest winters, but still does well at high elevations in the intermountain west.

This rockcress is similar to *Arabis caucasica* 'Variegata' in its need for good soil with excellent drainage and partial shade.

Irrigation requirements are also similar to other rockcresses. A deep irrigation once every seven to ten days works well. Yellow foliage is a definite sign of overwatering.

Mulch may be of organic material, such as compost, as long as drainage is good. Small gravel or rocks are also good mulches.

BLOOM

Flowers of this rockcress open on very delicate stems. Each flowering stalk is four to six inches, with several small white flowers. While there is a progression of bloom, this rockcress is similar to others with most flowers opening at the same time. The fragrance is not strong, but very pleasing up close. The bloom period is short in spring.

SEASONAL INTEREST

This miniature evergreen rockcress is attractive year-round. As a small-scale groundcover or as a container plant, *Arabis Ferdinandi-Coburgi* is an excellent accent for the winter garden.

COMPANION PLANTS AND LANDSCAPE USE

Use this lovely plant in small areas, choosing companions that will not compete. While the foliage colors are similar, green and white, I like to use *Arabis Ferdinandi-Coburgi* with the dwarf sedge, *Carex conica* 'Variegata'.

The miniature sweet flag, *acorus gramineus* 'Pusillus', with its yellow evergreen foliage is another grasslike plant that makes a nice companion in a container, between stepping stones, or in a small garden setting.

Viola labradorica is also a good companion, with a warning. This sweet little violet self-sows prolifically and may invade the rockcress if it has not yet filled in the area where it was planted.

On the west side of a large alder in my garden, I have a small patio area of stepping stones. Multiple small bulbs emerge in early spring: *Scilla, Puschkinia,* and *Galanthus.* They bloom before the tree leafs out fully, so they get plenty of sunlight. Nearby, the dwarf rockcress spreads contentedly, and gets shade protection from summer sun. Of course I have a bench in this area so that I can take time to enjoy these small treasures.

PROPAGATION

When rockcress is mature and growing vigorously it is often possible to remove a rooted rosette of foliage on a short stem.

Vegetative propagation also works during the growing season. Leave three to six leaves on the stem. This is your terminal bud and should root within four to six weeks.

MAINTENANCE

EASY! Removal of the faded flowers stalks will make the plant look tidier. However, if they are left on the plant after the flowers fade, the stalks soon collapse into the foliage.

Arabis procurrens
(rockcress)

Arabis procurrens

Arabis procurrens grows natively in southeastern Europe, and is my favorite rockcress for the garden. A vigorous evergreen, this rockcress spreads easily.

DESCRIPTION

Dark-green foliage forms evergreen rosettes typical of the rockcresses. Each stem supports several clusters. Individual leaves range in size from under one-half inch in the center of the rosette to an inch and a half. Each mature rosette is similar in size. Flowers are white, delicate, and lightly scented. *Arabis Sturii* (*A* x *sturii*) is related to *Arabis procurrens,* according to "Hortus Third". This little rock garden plant is low, under two inches, and very compact with a ten-inch spread.

CULTURAL REQUIREMENTS

Like the other rockcresses, *Arabis procurrens* is a mountain plant that adapts to many garden situations. I consider it to be the most vigorous of any rockcress, so if your garden climate seems demanding (very low or high humidity, hot summer temperatures, or winter cold) try this species.

Good soil with adequate compost, organic phosphorus and oyster shell is necessary. The compost is particularly important for aerating clay soils and increasing the water-holding capability of sandy soils.

Arabis procurrens will grow in full sun with regular irrigation once a week in my garden (clay loam). This is not a low-irrigation plant, but it does like good drainage, especially in winter.

Arabis procurrens will also take one of the toughest of garden exposures: full morning shade followed by hot afternoon sun.

Partial shade is a good exposure for this rockcress, but make sure it gets at least six hours of sun.

An organic mulch when you first plant *Arabis procurrens* is a good idea, so that it can spread easily. While it will spread in a gravel mulch, *Arabis procurrens* seems to be more vigorous with compost.

Irrigation once a week in the heat of the summer is best, though *Arabis procurrens* will tolerate more moisture.

BLOOM

Delicate white flowers on fine ten to twelve-inch stalks open in profusion in spring. The clear white against the dark-green foliage is quite striking. Another fragrant rockcress, *Arabis procurrens* spreads to cover two or three feet or more. The fragrance of this small-scale groundcover is notable a few feet away.

Bloom is in early spring and lasts a few weeks.

SEASONAL INTEREST

Arabis procurrens and *Arabis Sturii* are evergreens that look good year-round. In cold winter temperatures, the dark-green leaves are slightly bronzed, adding to the beauty of these plants.

An early bloomer, rockcress is a strong, attractive plant when much of the perennial garden is barely emerging from dormancy.

COMPANION PLANTS AND LANDSCAPE USE

Arabis procurrens will spread widely in a few years. One excellent use is near small shrubs such as *Spiraea japonica* 'Alpina'. As the shrub grows, the rockcress will grow around it, providing evergreen interest in the winter. A little shading from the ornamental shrub will not injure the rockcress.

Mid-sized ornamental grasses are also attractive companions. Blue sedge (*Carex glauca*) is an evergreen with fine, blue-green foliage that is beautiful against a mat of the dark-green *Arabis procurrens*.

While *Calamagrostis* species are larger ornamental grasses, a ground-cover of this rockcress at their base and surrounding areas makes each specimen of grass a focal point. Plant the *Arabis* two to three feet from the center of the *Calamagrostis.*

Species *Narcissus* planted as a drift or a clump near *Arabis procurrens* create a spring focal point when the two are in bloom together.

Arabis Sturii is so small that it should be used as an alpine with other small rock garden perennials: *Erinus alpinus* (alpine liver-balsam), *Saponaria pumilio* (alpine soapwort), *Achillea tomentosa* 'Moonlight' (creeping yarrow), or *Erysimum helveticum* (alpine wallflower). It may be used as a niche plant.

PROPAGATION

See *Arabis Fernandi-Coburgi.*

MAINTENANCE

See *Arabis Fernandi-Coburgi.*

Arabis procurrens

Arctostaphylos uva-ursi

ARCTOSTAPHYLOS

Arctostaphylos uva-ursi
(creeping manzanita)

This creeping evergreen manzanita is native from northern California into Alaska. Many cultivars have been discovered and named, but not all are deer-resistant. Included here are three I have grown in my garden that the deer have left alone. Also noted are the cultivars that have been consistently browsed or destroyed.

DESCRIPTION

Arctostaphylos uva-ursi is a vigorous evergreen groundcover that may reach a height of eighteen or more inches and a spread of ten feet. Small dark-green leaves on reddish stems almost hide the flowers. 'Point

Reyes' has slightly darker leaves than the species.

'Radiant' is a lighter and brighter green, and because leaves are spaced farther apart, the flowers are more visible. It grows lower to the ground, under one foot in height.

CULTURAL REQUIREMENTS

Creeping manzanita grows in cold areas of the western United States, including northern latitudes.

Full sun is the best exposure for *Arctostaphylos uva-ursi,* but it will also tolerate a little morning shade followed by hot afternoon sun. The cultivar 'Radiant' is tolerant of light shade.

Add compost to clay or sandy soils, but soil should not be too rich. Include plenty of organic phosphorus to encourage root growth, thus reducing the watering needs. Use oyster shell in acidic soils.

Good drainage, especially in winter, is essential. If the soil stays too moist, roots will rot partially or totally, eventually killing the plant.

Irrigation may not be necessary in cool-summer climates. In the Sierra foothills where I garden, summers are hot and dry (no fog!). Seldom is it cloudy. In our clay loam, irrigation once every three weeks is sufficient and may even be more than *Arctostaphylos uva-ursi* or 'Point Reyes' needs for survival. The cultivar 'Radiant' grows well with water every two to three weeks.

A mulch of organic material around the plant should not touch the primary stem, but should be spread to a distance of several feet from each plant. This will allow the prostrate stems to root, which will strengthen subsequent growth.

BLOOM

If you are familiar with the shape of heath blossoms, and then you will quickly recognize creeping manzanita as being in the same family (*Ericaceae*). Clusters of firm, pink, lantern-shaped flowers hang gracefully from short, red stems.

Early-summer bloom is followed by berries attractive to birds.

Arctostaphylos uva-ursi

Creeping manzanita is an attractive evergreen groundcover. In spring, as new growth starts, there is a contrast of greens within each plant. The red tones of the stems add another point of interest in all seasons.

Flowers hold for several weeks.

COMPANION PLANTS AND LANDSCAPE USE

Arctostaphylos uva-ursi, and the cultivars 'Radiant' and 'Point Reyes' are outstanding evergreen groundcovers for large areas. They should be combined with other robust perennials, subshrubs, or ornamental grasses.

The *Santolinas* are good as companion plants. My favorite companions, though, are the larger ornamental grasses. *Stipa gigantea* is beautiful as a single specimen in a sea of creeping manzanita.

In morning sun followed by afternoon shade, the cultivar 'Radiant' looks terrific with *Calamagrostis* 'Karl Forester'. Irrigate every two weeks.

Arctostaphylos uva-ursi

The creeping manzanitas are also good as single specimens in a rock garden, but do not allow them to overtake smaller rock garden treasures. Combine them with other strong perennial groundcovers: *Artemisia versicolor, Ceratostigma plumbaginoides* (dwarf plumbago), *Erigeron karvinskianus* (Santa Barbara daisy) and *Nepeta* 'Six Hills Giant'.

Slopes may be difficult to landscape, especially if they are in full sun sloping to a southern or a western exposure. *Arctostaphylos uva-ursi* is a good solution for this landscape challenge. See Introduction for commentary regarding landscaping a slope, and refer to Appendix 3 for a complete listing of companion plants.

PROPAGATION

Vegetative cuttings taken during the growing season are slow to root, but will increase your supply of plants.

Layering may work better. The ground under the end of a branch must be covered with a two-inch deep layer of organic mulch. Pin the creeping stems with a landscape staple near leaf nodes of this branching section, a few inches from the end. By fall the section should have rooted, allowing you to cut it from the parent plant and use it as a young start. This removal may also wait until spring.

MAINTENANCE

EASY! When plants are growing vigorously there is no maintenance necessary. Sometimes a cold winter will cause damage. Usually new spring growth will revitalize the plant. If sections appear to be severely damaged, remove them with a light pruning. Renew the mulch as needed.

Note: *Arctostaphylos* 'Emerald Carpet' is a cultivar of manzanita that has always been eaten by the deer in my garden. I have tried it several times. *Arctostaphylos* 'Massachusetts' and 'Wood's Compact' were also damaged, but I should try them both again.

Arctostaphylos uva-ursi 'Radiant'

Artemisia 'Powis Castle'

ARTEMISIA

Artemisia are wonderful low-irrigation groundcovers, mostly evergray, and a beautiful silver accent in the garden.

Artemisia 'Powis Castle' (*A.* 'Powys Castle')

This wormwood is a very attractive evergray subshrub for landscaping a southern or western exposure, including a slope. Several plants massed together, planted on four-foot centers, provide a stunning large-scale groundcover. For companion plants, refer to Appendix 3. For details about *Artemisia* 'Powis Castle' refer to "Deer in My Garden, Vol. 1".

Artemisia schmidtiana
(angel's hair)

Artemisia schmidtiana is a noninvasive wormwood, perfect for a small garden setting where a silver accent is desirable.

DESCRIPTION

The common name of angel's hair is apt for the soft, fine, silver foliage. New spring growth is very attractive. At maturity, this wormwood spreads to little more than one foot at the crown. However, its foliage and bloom stalks almost double the width. Height is eighteen inches to two feet.

The cultivar 'Silver Mound' is half the size of the species.

Flowers are typical of the *Artemisias,* a dull yellow. The primary color effect of the flower stalks is silver. Plants are dormant in winter in cold climates.

CULTURAL REQUIREMENTS

Angel's hair will grow in the coldest intermountain regions of the western United States. In areas of high humidity, it does not look as beautiful as it does in dry climates.

Full sun is the best exposure, but very light shade is tolerated as long as the soil is dry. Like other *Artemisias, A. schmidtiana* is undaunted by a western exposure.

Soil does not need to be rich, but clay soils should be amended with compost to improve drainage. Sandy soils need some compost to add nutrients and water-holding capability. All soils need an organic phosphorus when phosphorus levels are low.

Do not plant angel's hair where it will be in shade in winter.

Do not overwater. Foliage will yellow if the plants are over-irrigated. This indicator usually shows up in lower regions of the stem. Try not to water more than once every two weeks in clay loam. Even then, *Artemisia schmidtiana* should be planted on a dry edge of the border or rock garden.

Mulch with gravel or small rocks.

BLOOM

Small, dull-yellow flowers open on two-foot stalks in early summer. They may be used either as fresh cut flowers or as everlastings. The silver of the stalk is the dominant color for either usage. The flowers of angel's hair seem to detract from the beautiful mound of foliage. I usually prune them off as they form.

SEASONAL INTEREST

Angel's hair is a very attractive plant in early spring. If it is cut back a couple of times during the growing season, new foliage continues. While it may be evergray in milder climates, frequent rains in winter often spoil its appearance.

COMPANION PLANTS AND LANDSCAPE USE

Because it is not an aggressive grower, angel's hair may be used as an edging perennial or as an accent in the rock garden. Several plants grouped together may be used as a small-scale groundcover in dry areas of the landscape.

Santolina virens (green lavender cotton) is a wonderful companion plant, its rich dark-green foliage contrasting beautifully with the silver of *Artemisia schmidtiana. Salvia officinalis* 'Berggarten' has a blue-green cast to its gray foliage grown next to angel's hair, and the leaf size is definitely a pleasing contrast.

The blue tones of the fescues (Festuca) are also highlighted by the silver *Artemisia schmidtiana.*

Many of the cultivars in the *Thymus* genus are effective companion plants, especially those with bright or dark-green foliage.

Lavenders, too, with their shades of gray and gray-green, and purple flowers, are good companions with the bright-silver of angel's hair.

Artemisia schmidtiana will tolerate a very hot and dry exposure, and should be considered for gardens on a slope, especially when they are facing south or west. For companion plants in this challenging landscape situation, refer to Appendix 3.

Spring-flowering bulbs, including all *Narcissus* and *Allium* (these are deer-resistant) look even more beautiful with the silver foliage of this

Artemisia. Do not plant too closely, though, or the bulb foliage may overshadow the angel's hair.

PROPAGATION

Vegetative cuttings taken during the growing season root in three to four weeks. If you are using a cold frame or misting system, check the cuttings frequently. They must be planted as soon as possible after rooting, and moved to a drier location.

During the dormant season, divisions may be removed from the parent plant. Without disturbing its crown, dig into the soil at the edge of the plant, removing a rooted section. The entire plant may also be lifted and divided when it is not actively growing.

MAINTENANCE

No maintenance is necessary until late winter, when pruning back the plant almost to the crown will encourage beautiful new growth in early spring.

Flower stalks may be removed when they look spent.

Because I prefer the first flush of foliage growth, I frequently cut this plant back during the growing season. The first pruning occurs as blossom stalks form, the second when I feel the plant is looking rangy.

Artemisia versicolor 'Sea Foam'

One of my favorite groundcovers, *Artemisia versicolor* is an outstanding low-irrigation evergray in my rock garden.

DESCRIPTION

Lacy, silver foliage with a blue cast makes this perennial a highlight of the rock garden. A spreading plant that probably knows no bounds, this *Artemisia* has not been invasive in my garden. Its height is six to ten inches.

Flowers are inconspicuous, and form on twelve to fifteen-inch stalks that match the color of the foliage.

CULTURAL REQUIREMENTS

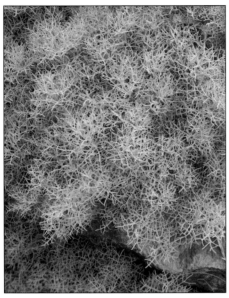

Artemisia versicolor

Same as for *Artemisia schmidtiana*. However, this *Artemisia* will tolerate light shade, making it possible to grow it in the vicinity of native oaks. I have also been able to grow it on the north face of a mounded rock garden area, where it gets full sun during the growing season but lower light in winter.

BLOOM

Flowers on this *Artemisia* look like tight buds on a silver stalk, appearing in early summer. The formation of flower stalks does not seem to detract from the appearance of *Artemisia versicolor*.

Use the flower stalks of this delicate *Artemisia* for fresh cut flowers or everlastings.

SEASONAL INTEREST

Prettiest during the growing season when its foliage is lush, *Artemisia versicolor* continues to be an attractive plant in the garden during the winter. In very cold winters, foliage may not be as full.

COMPANION PLANTS AND LANDSCAPE USE

I have noticed in my rock garden that this plant is particularly striking growing against a large rock. Rocks are the perfect foil for its delicate foliage.

Try this in a container with the evergreen ornamental grass *Helictotrichon sempervirens* (blue oat grass) for a pleasing contrast of blue and silver.

If you are landscaping a sloped hillside, especially if it faces west or south, *Artemisia versicolor* is a good choice. Spaced three feet apart, plants will soon fill in to cover a large area. For a listing of companion plants, refer to Appendix 3.

This is also a perfect small-scale groundcover for dry areas, or edges where sprinklers deliver little water.

Artemisia versicolor and *Cerastium Biebersteinii* mingled together (which they do when each grows into the other) are good companions.

PROPAGATION

Artemisia versicolor is very easy to propagate by vegetative cuttings taken during the growing season. They root in just a few weeks, and should be planted as soon as possible and moved to drier conditions.

Divisions may also be made by lifting a portion of the plant as it spreads. While I prefer to do this task during the dormant season, this is one tough perennial, and does not seem to mind when it's moved!

MAINTENANCE

VERY, VERY EASY! I usually prune some of the old growth from my stand of *Artemisia versicolor* just before it begins growth in late winter. But if I don't get this done, the plant still looks great. This is another reason to grow it on a slope that may be difficult to access.

Note: *Artemisia stelleriana* has been eaten by the deer in my garden.

Artemisia versicolor and *Cerastium Biebersteinii*

Asarum caudatum

ASARUM

The only ginger I have tried in my garden, *Asarum caudatum* was originally given to me by a friend who gardened in deer country. She was very excited about how well this had done in her garden. I planted the large divisions she brought me, and the deer promptly ate all of it the first night. It grew back, and they have never touched it since in more than ten years.

My summer climate may be too hot and dry to grow the ginger more suited to cold-winter climates, *Asarum canadense,* a native of the northeastern United States. It's possible that it may also be deer-resistant.

Asarum caudatum
(wild ginger)

Ginger is one of my favorite evergreen perennials for shade. Its large leaves and low growth make it very distinctive as a groundcover, or as an accent plant. In cold-winter areas it may be only semi-evergreen.

DESCRIPTION

Dark-green leaves are four to six inches long and wide. Each leaf grows from a stem originating at the crown of the plant as it spreads. *Asarum caudatum* is a strong spreader, but not invasive. Bloom is interesting, but not showy, in late spring.

CULTURAL REQUIREMENTS

Asarum caudatum will not survive in the coldest regions of the United States. It is native to the west coast.

An eastern exposure, filtered sunlight, and even deeper shade will all work for this wild ginger as long as the soil is fertile.

Enrich clay or sandy soils with lots of compost and organic phosphorus to encourage root growth. Add oyster shell in acidic soils.

Regular water once a week will encourage lush growth, which is most attractive. But *Asarum caudatum* will tolerate some drought if humidity is high and the plants are mulched with organic materials.

Keep the mulch renewed each year for vigorous growth.

BLOOM

My stand of *Asarum* seldom blooms, possibly because it grows in too much shade. When blossoms have emerged in early summer, each flower is small, on stems to six inches. Flowers are a brownish-purple and are not showy. They have an interesting bell shape with elongated tails, and are most notable up close.

SEASONAL INTEREST

Asarum caudatum is a beautiful evergreen groundcover year-round in my garden. I have it growing just outside one of the rooms in my house, a lovely view from the windows. Next to it is a shallow birdbath that brings frequent visitors (including raccoons who wash their paws after digging in my garden).

COMPANION PLANTS AND LANDSCAPE USE

Sarcococca hookerana humilis is an evergreen groundcover of a similar dark-green, but the leaves are very narrow. Grown near each other, the *Sarcococca* and the *Asarum* are a pleasing contrast in leaf form.

The lighter tones of *Lamium maculatum* provide more of a color contrast. Any one of the cultivars described would be a good companion plant for the *Asarum caudatum*.

Use the wild ginger as a small-scale groundcover for partial shade or shade. It will tolerate growing under trees where roots may be competitive. With ample compost and a good mulch, the *Asarum* will adapt.

As an accent plant or an evergreen in a container, *Asarum* is outstanding. Noteworthy because of its bold foliage and lush but tidy growth habit, it's a perfect edging plant, especially along a path.

PROPAGATION

Asarum caudatum should be propagated by divisions during the late fall, winter, or very early spring. Lift a portion of the plant and pull it apart gently.

MAINTENANCE

VERY EASY! No maintenance is necessary. Older plantings that do not seem to be growing vigorously may usually be renewed by simply adding mulch before new growth starts in the spring.

Aubrieta deltoidea

AUBRIETA

This sweet rock garden evergreen was named in recognition of Claude Aubriet (1668-1743) a French botanical artist. It grows in a broad region from southeastern Europe to western Asia. Fortunately, for rock garden enthusiasts, the two species detailed here have been made available in the horticultural trade.

Aubrieta deltoidea

Named for the petals which are shaped like the Greek letter delta, *Aubrieta deltoidea* is an evergreen with many variations. The one most frequently found in the nursery trade has purple flowers and gray-green leaves.

DESCRIPTION

The small gray-green leaves have an interesting shape, toothed at the tip. Stems are trailing, and when the plant is grown under ideal conditions, the leaves cover the stems, forming a mounding and trailing plant to eighteen inches in width, and under six inches in height, glorious in spring when it is covered with purple flowers.

CULTURAL REQUIREMENTS

Aubrieta deltoidea

Aubrieta deltoidea grows well in cold regions, including high elevations. It also does very well in the northwestern United States.

Full sun or very light shade are the best exposures for *Aubrieta.* I have even seen it spilling over a rock wall in a western exposure with reflected heat from a sidewalk.

Soil must be improved with compost, organic phosphorus, and oyster shell for calcium where soils are acidic.

Regular irrigation or rainfall is necessary once every seven to ten days in the first few years of growth. If grown in partial shade, watering every two weeks should be adequate in clay loam. *Aubrieta deltoidea* will tolerate drier conditions as a mature plant.

Drainage must be good in all seasons, but particularly in winter.

A mulch of organic materials is ideal, so that *Aubrieta deltoidea* has nutrients wherever it spreads.

BLOOM

While *Aubrieta deltoidea* includes cultivars in shades of rose, lavender, and purple, it is the bright-purple most commonly available in the nursery trade.

In spring, one-half inch diameter purple flowers bloom in profusion. The bloom period is short, lasting just a few weeks.

SEASONAL INTEREST

This is a nice evergreen (but slightly gray) rock garden plant. Spring is the height of its glory, but if *Aubrieta deltoidea* is cut back lightly after bloom, the plant remains attractive for the remainder of the season and into winter.

COMPANION PLANTS AND LANDSCAPE USE

I particularly like this rock garden plant used above a wall, allowing it to trail and spill over the edge. Useful also as a niche plant within rock walls, *Aubrieta deltoidea* may need to be cut back every year, so that it does not become rangy.

An outstanding companion is the early-blooming *Alyssum montanum* 'Mountain Gold', which blooms at the same time in my garden. Purple and gold are wonderful together! I also like to play the gray-green leaves and purple flowers against the silver of the *Artemisia* groundcovers.

Several plants spaced twelve inches apart make a nice small-scale groundcover.

Aubrieta deltoidea is effective as a container plant. This allows the gardener to move it into a special spot when it looks its best, and discreetly reposition the pot right after bloom when it is pruned back.

Use this *Aubrieta* near *Narcissus* or *Allium* bulbs.

PROPAGATION

Vegetative cuttings taken during the growing season after bloom root quickly. Cuttings taken in late May or early June will provide more plants for fall planting.

MAINTENANCE

EASY! *Aubrieta deltoidea* looks its best if it is pruned back slightly right after bloom fades. This will keep the foliage thicker so the plant will not look rangy. No maintenance is needed in late winter. In fact, it should not be pruned then because that would reduce the number of flowers in early spring.

Aubrieta gracilis

I found this evergreen rock garden treasure through the American Rock Garden Society. Drawn to its shiny bright-green leaves and compact appearance, I was not disappointed. This is one of my favorites of the smaller rock garden plants.

DESCRIPTION

Four-inch stems are covered with bright-green leaves, similar in shape to *Aubrieta deltoidea* with a toothed outer edge. The leaves are somewhat smaller on this *Aubrieta,* under three-eighths of an inch, forming small rosettes which add to the beauty of the plant.

The overall appearance of *Aubrieta gracilis* is a low, evergreen mound, under six inches in height. A mature plant has a spread of twelve to eighteen inches. Spring and early summer bring a show of periwinkle-blue flowers.

CULTURAL REQUIREMENTS

Aubrieta gracilis will grow in cold regions of the United States. Natively it is found in Greece and Albania.

Morning sun and afternoon shade is the best exposure. *Aubrieta gracilis* is less demanding of irrigation when grown in light shade, and the plant has a better appearance.

Full sun in my garden in the Sierra Nevada foothills is a successful exposure only when *Aubrieta gracilis* is watered frequently, at least once a week. I have even tried growing this perennial groundcover on a slight slope to the north (in full sun) where I was watering every two weeks, but it struggled with that low irrigation, probably because of the sun exposure in summer.

Soil should be amended with compost, organic phosphorus, and oyster shell where soils are acidic. An organic mulch helps maintain the vigor of the plant.

BLOOM

I love the color of the flowers of *Aubrieta gracilis!* I have no other plant in my garden that is this beautiful shade of periwinkle-blue with a hint of purple. Flowers open in late spring and early summer on three to four-inch stems held slightly above the foliage. The effect is striking.

Bloom continues for a few weeks, with multiple four-petaled flowers, each under half an inch, opening in progression. A few open at first, then the plant is covered with flowers, and finally a few more buds open for the finale.

SEASONAL INTEREST

An outstanding evergreen rock garden plant that needs little attention, *Aubrieta gracilis* is a winner in all seasons. Out of bloom it's a tidy mound of bright-green foliage. In bloom it glows with color. In winter its appearance is still excellent.

COMPANION PLANTS AND LANDSCAPE USE

Rock garden perennials needing similar exposure, soil preparation and irrigation requirements are perfect companions for the evergreen *Aubrieta gracilis*. This includes *Erinus alpinus* (alpine liver-balsam), *Erysimum helveticum* (alpine wallflower), *Saponaria pumilio* (soapwort), *Silene alpestris, Gypsophila cerastioides* (mouse-ears), *Sedum dasyphyllum, Sedum album* and *Scleranthus uniflorus*. All of these companions are also evergreen.

Though somewhat more aggressive in their growth habit, *Thymus serpyllum minus* (creeping thyme) and *Antennaria dioica* (pussy toes) are also good neighbors if kept a little at a distance.

With this wonderful list of companions, an enchanting rock garden could be created on a small scale using only a single specimen of each treasure. Add to this some very small bulbs (as long as the drainage is good), *Puschkinia, Scilla,* or species *Crocus* for a spring accent.

Use *Aubrieta gracilis* in a container. With a good soil mix and space for its roots to spread, it will do well for several years. Because it looks so good year-round, the container should be chosen carefully to complement the plant.

Aubrieta gracilis is a wonderful niche plant, planted in a rock wall as it is built. It will trail gracefully over the rocks without obscuring them. I would not use it between stepping stones, however, since it will spread and would be easily injured if people or animals were walking in the area.

PROPAGATION

Aubrieta gracilis is easy to propagate from vegetative cuttings taken during the more active growing season. Remove a rosette of leaves with about one-half an inch of stem. Carefully remove the lower leaves and insert the small cutting into a mix of one-half vermiculite and one-half perlite (see Introduction).

If the plant is spreading in a compost mulch, outer stems usually root very easily and may be removed without disturbing the primary plant.

MAINTENANCE

VERY, VERY EASY! I rarely groom my plant. However, faded flower stalks may be removed to improve the appearance of *Aubrieta gracilis* when the last bloom has faded. This may even prolong bloom when the plant is not putting energy into seed production.

Aubrieta gracilis

Campanula poscharskyana

Campanula is a large genus including many species of both groundcovers and taller perennials. The only *Campanula* left alone by the deer in my garden has been the evergreen *Campanula poscharskyana*.

Campanula poscharskyana
(Serbian bellflower)

This attractive evergreen groundcover is both beautiful and vigorous. Given space and good soil, it will continue to spread, covering a large area if encouraged to do so.

DESCRIPTION

Leaves are mid-green and slightly heart-shaped with toothed edges.

Campanula poscharskyana is a low groundcover, under eight inches, but its appearance is very lush and thick. In bloom, Serbian bellflower is taller as the flower stalks reach above and then bend over the foliage. Spread is very strong but not invasive. Each plant may spread to three feet or more.

CULTURAL REQUIREMENTS

Campanula poscharskyana will grow in the coldest regions of the western United States. It is very cold-tolerant, and while snows may flatten it, Serbian bellflower soon springs to life as the snow melts.

Thriving in many exposures, including full sun in mild climates near the coast, Serbian bellflower also does well in partial shade. Too much shade will be at the expense of flowering. Dappled shade under a deciduous tree is perfect. Full sun in my hot-summer Sierra foothill climate is too much sun!

Once established, *Campanula poscharskyana* is fairly drought-tolerant in partial shade. Irrigation once every ten to fourteen days may be sufficient in clay loam. Gardeners with sandy soil should water *Campanula poscharskyana* once a week.

Mulch is critically important to stimulate growth when plants are young. It is also possible to mulch lightly each year during the late winter.

BLOOM

Star-shaped flowers with four petals under one inch in length open in succession along branched stalks. Blue-lilac is the most commonly seen color, but cultivars of lavender and of white are available.

At first the flower stalks are upright, but as they elongate, they droop gracefully over the foliage. At full bloom this groundcover seems immersed in its blooms.

The strongest bloom is in late spring and early summer. Bloom continues for several weeks, especially if some of the faded flowers are removed.

SEASONAL INTEREST

An outstanding groundcover in all seasons, *Campanula poscharskyana* always looks good. Even in the cold of winter, Serbian bellflower is one of the most attractive plants in the garden.

COMPANION PLANTS AND LANDSCAPE USE

Because of its vigorous growth *Campanula poscharskyana* can easily overtake neighboring plants. I prefer to use it at the base of shrubs such as *Choiysa ternata* (Mexican orange) and *Lonicera nitida* (box honeysuckle) cultivars. Or combine it with very strong perennials: *Helleborus* (hellebore) species or *Iris unguicularis* (winter iris).

Another landscape use is to accent the Serbian bellflower with clusters of *Leucojum aestivum* (summer snowflake), bulbs that are very attractive emerging in the sea of *Campanula poscharskyana*. Both thrive in the relatively dry shade under my alder tree where the tree roots are competitive for moisture and nutrients.

Grow Serbian bellflower near the large-leafed ginger *(Asarum caudatum)* for an attractive contrast in leaf size year-round. The shapes of the leaves are similar, which is a subtle echo.

Lamiastrum galeobdolon may be grown as a nearby groundcover if each plant is given its own space, a respectful distance from the other. If *Euphorbia amygdaloides* ssp. *robbiae* is used as a companion, there's no holding either back. Both are strong spreaders and may intermingle when planted as close neighbors. If that effect pleases you, let them intertwine. The spurge will grow above the bellflower. Both are attractive evergreens.

In a container, Serbian bellflower will thrive for a few years. Eventually, soil will need to be renewed and the plant divided to revitalize its growth in the container.

Campanula poscharskyana is a good slope plant for eastern exposures or partial shade. A strong grower, it will quickly spread as a small-scale groundcover. Often available in flats, plugs may be spaced eight inches apart for a quick fill, or space larger plants two to three feet apart.

An attractive biennial for new plantings of Serbian bellflower is forget-me-not *(Myosotis sylvatica)*. Eventually the bellflower will overtake it.

PROPAGATION

It is easiest to propagate *Campanula poscharskyana* from divisions. Lift a section of the plant and pull it gently apart. You will note fine roots along the spreading stems. Any section will give you a new plant. The smaller the section you divide or cut off, the longer it will take to spread. Larger sections will establish more quickly.

MAINTENANCE

EASY! I do nothing to maintain my stand of *Campanula poscharskyana*. Faded flowers stalks seem to disappear into the foliage. I have visited gardens where faded flowers were removed and the stalks continued to bloom for months. Someday I may have time to be a fussy gardener!

I do occasionally renew the mulch in winter, adding an inch of compost after the alder leaves have fallen into the bed.

Cerastium tomentosum

CERASTIUM

Evergreen (and evergray) *Cerastium* species have been found at very high elevations (to 10,000 feet) in European mountains. While I have grown only two in my garden in the Sierra foothills, I would expect others in this genus also to be deer-resistant.

Cerastium Biebersteinii (C. biebersteinii)
(snow-in-summer)

This delightfully beautiful evergray *Cerastium* is one of my favorite rock garden plants. It was named after Friedrich August Marschall von Bieberstein (1768-1826), a German botanist.

DESCRIPTION

More compact than the closely related *Cerastium tomentosum*, *Cerastium Biebersteinii* is much lower (under six inches) and less rampant in its spread. While a single plant will continue to spread given the space, it is not aggressive. White flowers on short stems open in late spring as *Cerastium tomentosum* is finishing bloom.

Leaves of *Cerastium Biebersteinii* are white and woolly, smaller than those of *Cerastium tomentosum*.

CULTURAL REQUIREMENTS

Cerastium Biebersteinii

Cerastium is cold and heat-tolerant. It adapts to a wide range of garden situations.

Soil does not need to be rich, but the addition of compost in sandy or clay soils will improve tilth (see Introduction). Organic phosphorus will ensure strong roots. Also add oyster shell in acidic soils.

Good drainage is essential. This may be accomplished both by the addition of compost and by the placement of the plant in the correct exposure. Full sun year-round is optimal. While *Cerastium Biebersteinii* will tolerate very light shade, its form is most attractive when the plant is grown in full sun.

A mature *Cerastium Biebersteinii* is very drought-tolerant. In my rock garden in clay loam, this plant receives water once every two weeks. I have reduced the watering to once every three weeks with no ill effects.

Frequent watering may damage the plant, first causing lower leaves to yellow. This may be followed by stem rot and eventual decline of the plant. If you garden in a region where rains are frequent in summer, humidity very high, or the climate is cool and moist, this xeriphytic perennial may be difficult to grow. A gravelly soil may help, and reflected heat from nearby rocks will also create a warmer and drier microclimate.

Avoid organic mulches. They may keep the soil surface moist for too long after irrigation. Instead use gravel or small rocks as a mulch in all climates.

BLOOM

Bright-white flowers open on three to four-inch stalks in late spring. Perhaps because the stalks are short, they are more upright than the stalks of *Cerastium tomentosum*.

The bloom of *Cerastium Biebersteinii* begins just as *Cerastium tomentosum* finishes, extending the bloom season of snow-in-summer for a few more weeks.

Flowers may be used in very tiny fresh arrangements. I love to press the flowers and the foliage of this plant. In the middle of winter, I make pressed flower cards, using this white on purple or dark-green cardstock. Lovely!

SEASONAL INTEREST

A beautiful plant year-round, *Cerastium Biebersteinii* is a focal point in my rock garden. Even without the beautiful blossoms, this snow-in-summer has such beautiful form and unusual white foliage that it seems to be in bloom in all seasons.

COMPANION PLANTS AND LANDSCAPE USE

The white of the foliage is a great contrast with other perennials preferring good drainage in full sun. If a combination of low-growing plants is desirable, pair *Cerastium Biebersteinii* with *Teucrium cossonii* ssp.

majoricum (trailing germander), *Nepeta* species (catmint), or *Rosmarinus officinalis* 'Lockwood de Forest' or *R.* 'Prostratus' (trailing rosemary).

Subshrubs offer excellent choices of companions: all species and cultivars of *Lavandula* (lavender), *Santolina* (lavender cotton), and *Salvia officinalis* (sage). When the white foliage is played against the blue-green, gray-green, silver, or green foliage of the subshrub, who needs flowers?

Since containers are available in such beautiful color choices, planting a single *Cerastium Biebersteinii* in a special pot will be a perfect year-round accent for a hot, dry location. Place it, if possible, where you will see it from inside the house as well. This accent will glow in the sun, and still shine in the moonlight.

Cerastium Biebersteinii may be used as a small-scale groundcover, or planted eighteen inches apart they may spread to cover a larger area.

This tough plant is excellent for southern and western slopes. For a list of companions in this landscape situation see Appendix 3.

PROPAGATION

Vegetative cuttings taken during the growing season will root easily, and must not be left in humid conditions once they have rooted.

Divisions may also be taken late fall, winter, and early spring. Try to take them before new growth starts in the spring. The best season for divisions is in late fall, when you can lift a section of the plant and pull it apart to make as many divisions as possible. Check for roots in each section before planting.

MAINTENANCE

VERY EASY! I do very little to maintain my *Cerastium Biebersteinii*. Spent flowers stalks fade into the foliage and the snow-in-summer puts on a spurt of growth following bloom, covering the remains.

Faded flowers may be cut back, but this does not seem to affect a continuation of bloom.

Cerastium tomentosum
(snow-in-summer)

This evergray species of snow-in-summer, occasionally referred to as dusty miller (a common name used for other genera as well), is indigenous in Sicily and in the central and southern Apennines, to 6500-foot elevation.

DESCRIPTION

Gray-green leaves of this snow-in-summer are larger than the leaves of *Cerastium Biebersteinii.* Stems are also longer, to one foot or more. The overall effect is that of a billowing, spreading plant.

Multiple white flowers on branched stalks to one foot cover the plant in late spring.

CULTURAL REQUIREMENTS

Cerastium tomentosum

See *Cerastium Biebersteinii.*

Cerastium tomentosum will tolerate very light shade, making it a good choice for planting under native oaks. In my experience, its growth habit is similar in sun or light shade, but it should be watered even less frequently if it does not have full sun all day.

In my clay loam, plants have survived with water only once a month in the heat of the summer. I have also used this plant in my herbaceous border on a dry edge, where it mingles with taller perennials.

In the rock garden on a western slope, *Cerastium tomentosum* has done well for several years with a summer irrigation once every two weeks.

Use gravel or small rocks for mulch rather than organic materials. See *Cerastium Biebersteinii.*

COMPANION PLANTS AND LANDSCAPE USE

See *Cerastium Biebersteinii*. In using the same companions, remember that *Cerastium tomentosum* is larger (taller and more exuberant) and may climb into the subshrubs or adjacent groundcovers. This one likes to mingle!

Because it is rangy by nature, I would use this one only in a very large container combined with other plants. Use it with the evergreen *Helictotrichon sempervirens* (blue oat grass). A light shearing after bloom will encourage new growth on the *Cerastium* and keep it looking more attractive.

This enthusiastic perennial is an excellent choice for a large-scale groundcover, especially on a slope. While it doesn't need any maintenance when it's grown in full sun, a weedeater or a mower may be used to cut it back after bloom and encourage fresh new growth.

Refer to Appendix 3 for a list of companions suited to western and southern slopes in full sun.

PROPAGATION

See *Cerastium Biebersteinii*.

MAINTENANCE

EASY! The only maintenance that is desirable with mature plants is to remove old growth and encourage new. Do this with a light shearing or serious mowing right after bloom. Plants may be cut back to ground level. They will regrow quickly.

CERATOSTIGMA

Ceratostigma plumbaginoides
(dwarf plumbago)

Though dormant in winter, and late to begin growth in spring, *Ceratostigma plumbaginoides* has attracitve foliage, blue flowers in late summer, and great fall colors. For details, see "Deer in My Garden, Vol. 1".

This genus, a member of the *Compositae* family (daisies), includes several wonderful species and cultivars that are deer-resistant. The species detailed here is chosen only because it is low to the ground, and commonly used as a groundcover.

Chamaemelum nobile (Anthemis nobilis)
(Russian chamomile, garden chamomile)

It is interesting to note that this evergreen plant is indigenous to western Europe and northern Africa. The name is from the Greek chamai (on the ground) and melon (this refers to the fruity scent of the foliage and its low habit of growth). This is not the chamomile herb used for tea; that plant is *Matricaria recutita* (*M. chamomilla*).

DESCRIPTION

Very finely-cut light-green leaves are lacy in appearance, but grow thickly to form a low evergreen mat under three inches in height. In optimal conditions, *Chamaemelum nobile* will continue to spread relentlessly. Soil fertility, climate conditions, and irrigation practices will determine both the thickness and the height of chamomile.

'Flore Pleno' is a blooming cultivar with white daisies. 'Treneague' is a nonflowering cultivar, and often the preferred choice for a lawn since it needs no mowing to keep it low.

CULTURAL REQUIREMENTS

Chamaemelum nobile is a vigorous plant in many zones. Strength in winter will be determined by snow cover and availability of winter sun. Where I garden in the Sierra foothills, a few feet of snow will usually melt within a week. Chamomile emerges unscathed. However, if it is in low winter light, and we have our frequent heavy rains accompanied by cold, this usually evergreen plant may die back a bit.

Chamomile will grow well in full sun or partial shade.

Soil does not need to be rich, but it should be amended with compost, organic phosphorus, and oyster shell in acidic soils.

A compost mulch is beneficial, especially in new plantings. This will give the chamomile a loose and fertile surface upon which to spread.

BLOOM

Chamomile blooms in spring and summer with small white daisies. Some are little more than a yellow button of a flower, with short white rays. Other cultivars have pretty daisies on fine stems to six inches. One common chamomile has drooping white rays. 'Flore Pleno' has distinctly larger flowers that are nice for small cut flower arrangements.

Chamomile may stop blooming in summer heat. If it is mowed, that may encourage more flowering with the new growth, but usually on shorter stalks.

SEASONAL INTEREST

In most climates, *Chamaemelum nobile* is evergreen, and a pretty groundcover year-round. However, in clay soils with extended cold and wet conditions, there may be partial die-back.

In spring, the blooming cultivars are attractive as groundcovers, especially mingled with other low plants.

COMPANION PLANTS AND LANDSCAPE USE

Chamomile is a strong grower that may be used on its own as a groundcover in a large or small area. In small gardens, it may need to be restrained from spreading into other plants.

Chamaemelum nobile is also an excellent lawn substitute, especially when it is combined with other low-growing tough plants: *Viola labradorica* (Labrador violet), *Prunella vulgaris* (self-heal), *Thymus serpyllum* (creeping thyme), and even *Achillea millefolium* (common yarrow) when it is mowed.

In a small container, a bit of chamomile provides an interesting addition for a deck or small garden patio area, where people young and old will be inspired to touch and smell it.

PROPAGATION

Chamaemelum nobile is easily propagated from vegetative cuttings taken during the growing season. However, it is also very easy from divisions.

Lift a section of the plant, checking for roots. This propagation is best done in spring or fall.

MAINTENANCE

EASY! The nonblooming 'Treneague' needs no maintenance. Blooming cultivars of chamomile benefit from being mowed as blooms fade. This will make the plant tidier and denser. And it may even encourage a few more flowers.

If established stands of chamomile seemed to have lost their vigor, mow close to the ground, then spread a half an inch of light compost. New growth should be just as bright and beautiful as it was when young.

Coreopsis verticillata 'Moonbeam'

COREOPSIS

Coreopsis verticillata 'Moonbeam'

This low-growing *Coreopsis* is an excellent addition to the genre of groundcovers and rock garden perennials. It will be dormant in winter. For details, see "Deer in My Garden, Vol. 1".

Cotoneaster apiculatus 'Tom Thumb'

COTONEASTER

A large genus of shrubs and shrubby groundcovers, *Cotoneaster* includes several species the deer love and, fortunately, a few they ignore.

Cotoneaster apiculatus 'Tom Thumb'
(dwarf cranberry cotoneaster)

This lovely deciduous cotoneaster from China has been growing in a container at my nursery entrance for more than ten years. It is the only cultivar in the species that I have grown and tested for deer-resistance.

DESCRIPTION

The stiff branches of 'Tom Thumb' have a slight draping habit, forming a mound under two feet in spread, and under six inches in height. Dark-green leaves are less than one-fourth inch in length and spaced alternately along flattened branching stems, creating a delicate effect. Small white flowers under one-fourth inch open in early summer. Fall brings beautiful color to the tiny leaves.

CULTURAL REQUIREMENTS

See *Cotoneaster microphyllus.*

BLOOM

The blooms are not as noticeable as those of *Cotoneaster microphyllus.* They are quite small and mostly solitary. The overall effect is that of delicate rather than abundant bloom.

Flowers are followed by soft-red berries, notable in fall and winter.

SEASONAL INTEREST

Cotoneaster apiculatus 'Tom Thumb'

Because this plant is not evergreen, its strongest seasons of interest are in spring with new growth, summer with flowers, and fall with foliage color change. My favorite season is in the fall when reds and golds are the dominant color, mingled with the soft-red of the tiny berries.

The branching habit makes this an interesting plant in the winter garden even though it has no leaves during the dormant season. Dusted with snow, this dormant plant adds a picturesque pattern in the landscape.

COMPANION PLANTS AND LANDSCAPE USE

This *Cotoneaster* is somewhat smaller than *Cotoneaster microphyllus,* and its uses in the landscape differ. It may be used as a singular accent plant in a small garden or several plants grouped together as a groundcover.

Companion plants must be chosen carefully so they do not overtake this smaller *Cotoneaster.* Tight creeping thymes are good choices where irrigation is at least as frequent as once every two weeks. *Antennaria dioica* (pussy toes) and *Cerastium Biebersteinii* (snow-in-summer) also work well as companions to 'Tom Thumb' in a low-irrigation landscape. *Artemisia versicolor* may be considered too rampant a grower as a companion.

Cotoneaster apiculatus 'Tom Thumb' thrives in an eastern exposure, but it's also rugged enough for a southern or western slope. Draping over a rock wall, it is beautiful, even in winter when there are no leaves.

A perfect container plant, *Cotoneaster* 'Tom Thumb' may be moved into full view when its color is so delightful in fall.

PROPAGATION

See *Cotoneaster microphyllus.*

MAINTENANCE

VERY, VERY EASY! *Cotoneaster* 'Tom Thumb' needs no maintenance. You don't even need to rake up the fallen leaves, because they add to the mulch. Just enjoy!

Cotoneaster thymifolius

Cotoneaster microphyllus
(rockspray cotoneaster)

Cotoneaster microphyllus is an evergreen from the Himalayas and southwest China. Perhaps it is the very tiny leaves of this cotoneaster that keep the deer from being interested.

DESCRIPTION

Cotoneaster microphyllus is a small-leafed shrubby evergreen that branches low to the ground with a two to three-foot height, spreading to six feet. Leaves are dark-green and little more than a quarter of an inch. The subspecies *Cotoneaster microphyllus thymifolius* has even smaller leaves, slightly rolled under. Both bloom with small white flowers followed by tiny soft-red berries.

CULTURAL REQUIREMENTS

Cotoneaster microphyllus

Cotoneaster microphyllus is tolerant of cold climates, including the mountain and intermountain regions of the western United States. It also grows well in mild climates.

Rockspray cotoneaster thrives in full sun and will also tolerate partial shade. Because it does well with low irrigation, this plant is a good choice for growing in the partial shade of native oaks.

Soil does not need to be rich, but it should be improved with compost in both clay and sandy soils. Add organic phosphorus for good root development, and oyster shell in acidic soils to make the nutrients available to the plants.

Cotoneaster microphyllus will tolerate regular irrigation once a week, but does not need it. In clay loam, a deep irrigation once every two to three weeks is adequate. In fertile soil with a thick mulch of decomposing straw, a mature rockspray cotoneaster is very drought-tolerant and may survive with watering only once a month, especially in partial shade.

Mulch should be of organic materials to add nutrients and conserve moisture in the soil. A three-inch deep layer of straw, or a mix of compost, leaves, and straw is ideal.

BLOOM

White flowers are tiny, less than one-fourth of an inch. The bloom is attractive, with multiple flowers opening along the branching stems of the plant in late spring. Berries follow the flowering, turning to a soft-red by fall.

SEASONAL INTEREST

A shrubby evergreen, *Cotoneaster microphyllus* looks good year-round. Each season brings a change: new growth in early spring followed by a profusion of white flowers, green berries and lush growth in summer, berries turning to a soft-red in fall and lingering into winter.

This plant is beautiful when a bit of snow falls, caught on its angular branches and small leaves.

COMPANION PLANTS AND LANDSCAPE USE

Both *Cotoneaster microphyllus* and the subspecies *Cotoneaster microphyllus thymifolius* are beautiful as single specimen plants in a rock garden. Used in this landscape situation, they may be surrounded by low groundcovers: species and cultivars of *Thymus* (thyme), *Artemisia versicolor* (wormwood), *Stachys* 'Silver Carpet' (lamb's ears), and *Cerastium Biebersteinii* (snow-in-summer).

Irrigate according to the plant with the greater need. For example, combining *Cotoneaster microphyllus* and green-leafed thymes will establish an irrigation schedule of deep watering once every two weeks. If the watering plan in the heat of the summer is once every three weeks, *Stachys* and *Cerastium* are good choices. Watering even more infrequently, use *Artemisia versicolor* as a companion, or the native *Antennaria dioica* (pussy toes).

Avoid interplanting with companion rock garden plants that may be overshadowed by the size *(Erinus alpinus, Erysimum helveticum, Alyssum tortuosum*). Rock garden plants needing full sun (*Dianthus*) will not be good companions either. The *Cotoneaster* may exclude light.

A large mass planting of *Cotoneaster microphyllus*, especially on a slope, is very attractive. The slope may be to the east, south, or even to the west, in full sun. Reflected heat from rocks, a wall, sidewalk, or even a hot asphalt driveway will not damage this tough plant. Refer to Appendix 3 for a listing of suitable companions.

In a large container that will allow sufficient space for good root development, rockspray cotoneasters are attractive accents. They may also be pruned to fit a small space.

PROPAGATION

Take vegetative cuttings of rockspray cotoneaster anytime during the growing season. They root easily, and taken in late spring may provide good planting material for fall planting.

Layering may also be done, and requires less work or attention. Using a landscape staple, pin one of the lower branches into the compost mulch. Place the staple at a joint of branching about twelve inches or less from the end of the branch. Add more compost (a small pile) on top. Rooting should occur in a few weeks if plants are irrigated. As temperatures cool in fall, cut off the rooted section and plant it in another location.

MAINTENANCE

VERY EASY! This *Cotoneaster* needs no maintenance. Renew the mulch as needed. Prune upright branches if a more horizontal form is desired.

Note: I have not grown *Cotoneaster microphyllus* 'Cooperi' in my garden, a cultivar with very small leaves, forming a mound twelve inches in width. I would expect it to be deer-resistant as well.

Cymbalaria muralis

CYMBALARIA

The name originates from the Greek kymbalon (a cymbal), which refers to the shape of the leaves. While there are several species of *Cymbalaria*, the only one I have grown in my garden in the foothills of the Sierra Nevada range in California is the one included here, which the deer have left alone.

Cymbalaria muralis
(Kenilworth ivy)

I first saw this sweet, trailing, semi-evergreen groundcover when I was wandering the backstreets of a gold rush town (Nevada City, CA) near where I live. Established in an old stone wall, the Kenilworth ivy looked as though it had been there as long as the wall, well over 100 years. Now I know that it may have been planted only last year!

DESCRIPTION

Cymbalaria muralis seems too delicate to describe as rambunctious or invasive. However, the reach of its spread is documented. A European native, Kenilworth ivy has naturalized from Ontario to Pennsylvania, and west to the Pacific Coast.

The light-green leaves are a pretty shape, with three to seven lobes. In fertile soil they may be an inch wide, but in most soils they are less. Delicate trailing stems root easily where they touch the growing medium, whether it is mulch or potting soil.

Cymbalaria muralis blooms in spring with small pale-lilac flowers.

CULTURAL REQUIREMENTS

Kenilworth ivy may not survive in very cold winters. In my garden, where temperatures in winter have dipped as low as 8° F with no snow cover, *Cymbalaria muralis* has not been damaged. It has also survived under three to four feet of snow with no appreciable change.

The best exposures are very bright but shady locations. A north wall that receives filtered sunlight is ideal. Some sun will be tolerated if irrigation is frequent.

Soil should be rich, but preparation does not need to be deep. This shallow-rooted groundcover spreads easily in a mulch of compost.

Cymbalaria muralis grows well when it receives regular irrigation. For that reason, in my dry climate it's happiest growing in my cold frame where the misters provide moisture three times a day for the propagation flats. Growing outside in a large container where it receives irrigation once a day, Kenilworth ivy is pretty but not as lush during my hot and arid summer.

Mulches should be organic materials: decomposed leaves or straw, compost, or a mix.

BLOOM

Flowers look like miniature snapdragons, pale-lilac with delicate purple markings (use a lens!), under half an inch in length. Each bloom is nestled into the delicate foliage on short stems. Bloom lasts for several weeks in spring, and may even continue into summer if the plant is growing in ideal conditions.

SEASONAL INTEREST

Cymbalaria muralis is evergreen in milder climates. Its leaves are so attractive, it is a nice plant in a container even when out of bloom.

COMPANION PLANTS AND LANDSCAPE USE

Because of its vigorous growth, *Cymbalaria muralis* may be expected to climb into any perennial you plant near it! Ornamental grasses for shade make good companions: *Carex flava* (gold sedge), *Carex conica* 'Variegata', (dwarf variegated sedge), and *Hakonechloa macra* 'Aureola' (Japanese forest grass).

In partial shade, *Carex glauca* (blue sedge) is very pretty with *Cymbalaria muralis,* especially when the latter is in bloom and the *Carex* foliage color echoes the color of the *Cymbalaria* flowers.

Helleborus species (hellebore) are also good companions. Since I prefer to grow *Cymbalaria muralis* in a container, the companions suggested have been chosen for their worth as container plants.

Kenilworth ivy may also be grown with ferns as companions.

Whether planted near a wall or in a container, Kenilworth ivy is most attractive given an opportunity to spill over the sides.

While growth is strong, I would not mass *Cymbalaria muralis* as a groundcover for shady areas because there are better choices of plants for covering the ground (*Lamium maculatum, Campanula poscharskyana, Sarcococca hookerana humilis,* and *Asarum caudatum*).

PROPAGATION

There's no need to work hard at propagating Kenilworth ivy. It seems to be able to find its own way. Small sections root easily in moist soil. Or reach into the center of a mass of *Cymbalaria muralis* and remove a larger section with roots.

Seed is very tiny, but *Cymbalaria* will self-sow if the seed drops on a loose surface such as compost or small gravel.

MAINTENANCE

If old growth is too rangy, cut back the plant to encourage new growth. Add a little compost after cutting back the plant, and it should respond with more attractive foliage.

DELOSPERMA

The only *Delosperma* I have tried in the garden is the hardy South African rock garden plant. Other species may not be as hardy and may be eaten by the deer.

Delosperma nubigenum 'Lesotho'
(hardy ice plant)

A friend who gardens where there are serious deer problems thought this would be a good addition to my garden. I've grown it for several years and the deer have not bothered it. It's possible that other tight species may also be left alone.

DESCRIPTION

Delosperma nubigenum 'Lesotho' is a succulent plant, though it is not a hardy sedum. The plump leaves are under half an inch in length, a beautiful bright-green. Some take on a red cast with winter cold.

Height is under one inch and spread to three feet with very tight growth. Bright golden-yellow flowers are plentiful in late spring.

CULTURAL REQUIREMENTS

This hardy ice plant has been tested to 8°F in my garden. Snow cover or no snow cover, the foliage of *Delosperma nubigenum* 'Lesotho' may change color, but it is not damaged.

Full hot sun in my Sierra foothill garden was too much for this plant! Planted on the east side of a large rock, it grows much better. Just a little bit of afternoon shade makes a difference.

Soil should have compost and organic phosphorus added, but it should not be rich, and preparation does not need to be deep. Gardeners with acidic soil should also add oyster shell (see Introduction).

Similar to hardy sedums, *Delosperma nubigenum* 'Lesotho' thrives where it gets irrigation once a week. With a gravel mulch to spread into, irrigation may be reduced to once every ten to fourteen days.

BLOOM

One-inch daisies with multiple thin petals shine with color. The golden-yellow flowers almost cover the foliage when the plant is in bloom. Bloom lasts for three to four weeks in late spring and early summer. When the flowers fade, they disappear into the plant.

COMPANION PLANTS AND LANDSCAPE USE

Choose companions carefully. Plants should not overshadow this low groundcover. Any one of the hardy sedums listed in Appendix 2 would be pretty growing nearby, but give each one the appropriate amount of space in which to spread.

For example, *Sedum dasyphyllum,* with its blue foliage, would be a nice contrast. The spacing between each plant should be two to three feet unless you plan to dig them up within a couple of years.

Sedums and *Delosperma* may also be grown in a container, including a strawberry pot, where their trailing habit and foliage color is accented by the container.

Delosperma nubigenum 'Lesotho' is a wonderful small-scale groundcover.

PROPAGATION

Propagation of this hardy ice plant is very easy. Small sections placed on gravel will usually root right in the garden. Cuttings may also be placed on top of a vermiculite and perlite mix with only a very small portion of stem. They will soon root!

MAINTENANCE

VERY, VERY EASY! This lovely groundcover needs no maintenance.

Dianthus

DIANTHUS

This genus has a large number of species and cultivars. As I tried several of them over the last 30 years, I observed that the deer will damage most cultivars of *Dianthus deltoides* and *Dianthus plumarius,* eating the flowers and ripping into the foliage.

Continuing frustration with trying to grow the traditional cottage pinks with deer in my garden inspired me to search further in this genus of delightfully fragrant plants. Membership in the American Rock Garden Society was both an opportunity for education and the means of finding rarer selections of *Dianthus.*

Dianthus which are very tight in their growth habit are left alone by the deer. Both the flowers and the evergreen foliage are untouched. Because of their similarities, all the *Dianthus* are grouped together here, with differences noted in their description.

DESCRIPTION

All species described are evergreen.

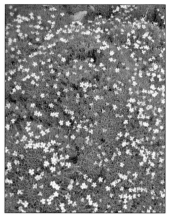

Dianthus erinaceus

Dianthus erinaceus: The oldest alpine *Dianthus* (fourteen years) in my rock garden, *Dianthus erinaceus* has spread to three feet. Its gray-green foliage is tiny, less than one-eighth of an inch, forming a dense mat under three inches in height. In late spring, tiny, pink, singular flowers open in profusion for a few weeks.

Dianthus gratianopolitanus (cheddar pink): The foliage of this rock garden pink is blue-green, with individual leaves to one-half inch, giving it a softer appearance than *Dianthus erinaceus*. One cultivar is 'Tiny Rubies' with very fragrant, deep rosy-pink flowers on three to four-inch stems. The species also has other selections of pink. Flowers are about one-half inch. Spread is two to three feet. Height out of bloom is under two inches, and in bloom to four inches.

Dianthus gratianopolitanus

Dianthus microlepsis: Fragrant flowers (one-half inch) on a more compact plant are typical of this alpine species. Foliage is gray-green with foliage one-half inch to three-fourths inch. Growing in a mound, this small alpine may spread to one foot. 'Albus' is a cultivar with white flowers.

Dianthus petraeus ssp. noeanus: This extraordinary rock garden pink is the last to bloom, opening its lacy and very fragrant white flowers in late June and early July in my garden. Flower stalks are four to six inches in height, and individual flowers to one-inch width. Foliage is gray-green and individual leaves to three-fourths inch have very sharp ends.

Dianthus simulans: A small alpine pink, *Dianthus simulans* has gray-green foliage, with dense growth forming a mound under two inches in height. Small pink flowers on short stems bloom close to the foliage. Spread is to one foot.

Dianthus squarrosus: Another alpine treasure, this pink is under three inches in height and spreads to one foot. Green leaves are three-fourths inch in length, forming a grassy tuft. Small, fringed, very fragrant white flowers on four to five-inch stems are held above the foliage.

CULTURAL REQUIREMENTS

Dianthus petraeus ssp. *noeanus*

Dianthus are found in cold mountain regions in their native habitat. These are hardy evergreens. While I have not tried it in my garden, the species *Dianthus glacialis* has been found near the glaciers in the Alps.

Dianthus species described here must have full sun! They will not tolerate any shade, including the shade of a rock. If planted near a rock, *Dianthus* must be on the south side.

Soil should not be rich, but add some compost to clay or sandy soils. The addition of organic phosphorus will ensure good root development, and oyster shell must also be added in acidic soils.

Irrigation once every two weeks in clay loam is appropriate during the heat of the summer. I have irrigated less frequently (every three weeks), and the *Dianthus* in my rock garden have still done well. Do not overwater! *Dianthus* must have good drainage in all seasons.

A gravel mulch is better than an organic mulch which may cause rotting of the lower foliage. If you garden in an area of higher humidity, placing small rocks near the *Dianthus* may change the microclimate to hotter and drier.

BLOOM

Dianthus gratianopolitanus with *Salvia* 'Berggarten'

As described above, *Dianthus* flowers vary in color with shades of pink, rose, and white. Most are fragrant, and some are more intensely so. Bloom begins in my garden in May and continues for a few weeks. *Dianthus petraeus* ssp. *noeanus* is the last to bloom in late June and early July.

Cultivars of *Dianthus gratianopolitanus* may have more continuous bloom if they are deadheaded as blooms fade.

The species with longer stalks may be used for cut flowers, though arrangements will be small.

SEASONAL INTEREST

Because they are evergreen, the species and cultivars of *Dianthus* described here are beautiful alpine and rock garden plants year-round. The flowers are an added bonus of fragrance and beautiful color in late spring and early summer.

Dianthus do not change with winter cold. Since they need as much winter sun as possible, the beautiful foliage of this genus should lure you into the garden on a cold winter day.

COMPANION PLANTS AND LANDSCAPE USE

Each one of the *Dianthus* I have grown is a good companion to another. There is certainly enough contrast in foliage and flower form, color, and even size if they are all grown in proximity. Remember to allow for the spread of each in distance apart when planting. *Dianthus* may not be moved easily when mature.

Gypsophila repens (creeping baby's breath) is another good companion since it blooms about the same time. Its habit is more trailing, so be careful to plant it three to four feet from the *Dianthus*.

Several plants of *Dianthus gratianopolitanus* may be planted one foot apart for a small-scale groundcover.

Alpine troughs are perfect planters for *Dianthus simulans* and *Dianthus squarrosus* because these species stay so small. *Alyssum tortuosum* could be added as a companion.

All the *Dianthus* may be grown in containers as long as the containers are in full sun.

PROPAGATION

Vegetative propagation is the best way to increase your supply of plants. Cuttings may be taken during the growing season even when the plant is in bloom. They root quickly.

MAINTENANCE

Dianthus squarrosus with *Erinus alpinus*

VERY, VERY EASY! Deadheading may be done on those cultivars and species with longer flowering stalks to improve the plant appearance and prolong bloom. The species with very tiny flowers, *Dianthus erinaceus* does not lose its beauty as flowers fade and disappear into the foliage.

Erigeron karvinskianus

Erigeron karvinskianus
(Santa Barbara daisy, fleabane)

Erigeron karvinskianus is a beautiful, semi-evergreen groundcover. It may be used as a single specimen plant and serves as a companion to many of the rock garden perennials in this volume. It is also an excellent edging plant, though it is dormant in winter. For details, refer to, "Deer in My Garden, Vol. 1".

Euphorbia amygdaloides ssp. *robbiae*

EUPHORBIA

Euphorbia amygdaloides ssp. *robbiae*
(Mrs. Robb's bonnet, wood spurge)

Euphorbia cyparissias
(cypress spurge)

Both these species of *Euphorbia* make excellent groundcovers for large areas, since they are very strong spreaders.

For detailed information refer to "Deer in My Garden, Vol. 1".

Galium odoratum

Galium odoratum
(sweet woodruff)

Galium is a vigorous, deciduous groundcover for partial shade. It is a beautiful small-scale or large-scale groundcover, and an excellent edging plant. For detailed information, refer to "Deer in My Garden, Vol. 1".

Geranium sanguineum

Geranium x cantabrigiense

Geranium x cantabrigiense 'Biokovo'

Geranium sanguineum
'Cedric Morris'

Hardy geraniums are attractive groundcovers, edgers, or specimens for an irrigated garden in partial shade. Refer to "Deer in My Garden, Vol. 1" for detailed information.

Gypsophila repens
(creeping baby's breath)

These semi-evergreen alpine natives from Europe are beautiful delicate trailing plants for the rock garden.

DESCRIPTION

Narrow leaves are gray-green, under one inch in length and spaced apart on delicate branching stems. Out of bloom the plant is not strong in form, nor is the foliage strong in color. In bloom the plants are notable. The white cultivar 'Alba' trails more than the pink 'Rosea', and also blooms longer.

Height of a mature plant is under one foot. 'Alba' may trail to as much as two to three feet. 'Rosea' has a spread of about eighteen inches.

CULTURAL REQUIREMENTS

Gypsophila repens will grow in the coldest regions of the United States. It is found indigenously from 4000 to more than 8500-foot elevation in the Alps, Pyrenees, and Apennines.

Full sun is the best exposure for maximum bloom. Any shade tends reduce flowering, though with at least six hours of sunlight, *Gypsophila repens* is still a beautiful accent.

Improve soil with compost and organic phosphorus for best growth and flowering. Add oyster shell in acidic soils. *Gypsophila* does well in rocky soils as long as compost has been added.

Irrigation may be frequent, once a week, or it may be more infrequent. In my rocky clay loam, watering once every two weeks has been adequate. This plant has a deep root system.

Mulches may be organic materials, gravel, or small rocks. Creeping baby's breath benefits from the reflected heat of nearby rocks.

BLOOM

Delicate branching stems with many buds continue to develop for several weeks, extending the bloom from early to midsummer. If faded flowering stalks are removed when they are totally through blooming, more buds may emerge.

Flowers are delicate, under one-half inch, but there are so many that the plant is quite showy.

'Alba' is longer blooming than 'Rosea', often continuing its bloom into late summer, even without deadheading.

SEASONAL INTEREST

Though the gray-green foliage is very pretty when the plant is growing strongly in early spring, its strength as a landscape plant is during bloom, especially when several plants are massed together.

COMPANION PLANTS AND LANDSCAPE USE

Gypsophila repens makes a nice edging for a larger flower border or along a path or walk. Single plants may be used as an accent edging, or several may be grouped together for a stronger statement.

A rock wall is a perfect place to use *Gypsophila repens,* where it should be planted above the wall and allowed to trail over it.

Creeping baby's breath rambling through and around small ornamental grasses is very attractive. Choose grasses with compatible light, soil, and irrigation requirements: *Bouteloua gracilis* (grama grass), *Festuca* (fescue), and *Stipa tenuissima* (feather grass).

Gypsophila repens may be used in a container alone or with one of the grasses mentioned above. It may also be combined with the annual alyssum, and the two allowed to trail together. Combine the pink creeping baby's breath with white and purple annual alyssum!

PROPAGATION

Gypsophila repens is easily propagated from vegetative cuttings taken during the growing season, even when the plant is in bloom. Cuttings of terminal buds must be nonflowering growth.

MAINTENANCE

EASY! In late winter, I cut the entire plant back to the crown. However, if this maintenance is not done the plant will still put on nice new growth in the spring.

Herniaria glabra
(rupturewort)

An evergreen perennial native to Europe and the Mediterranean region in particular, *Herniaria glabra* is one of two species of rupturewort. The second, *Herniaria alpina,* is probably also deer-resistant, but I have not grown it in my garden.

DESCRIPTION

Herniaria is an evergreen trailing herb that does well as a groundcover. Foliage is quite crowded on branching stems, with small, bright-green leaves one-eighth inch or slightly more in length. Tiny, white flowers are inconspicuous.

Rupturewort hugs the ground as it grows, and is seldom more than two inches in height. Spread of a single plant may be three feet or more.

CULTURAL REQUIREMENTS

In very cold climates, *Herniaria glabra* is not a perennial herb. However, it certainly does well in many cold areas, withstanding winter temperatures to 20°F.

Full sun in my garden climate in the western foothills of the Sierra Nevada range is too hot an exposure for *Herniaria glabra.* It grows beautifully in the spring and then begins to burn in the heat of the summer. Partial shade is the best exposure. In milder climates, especially where clouds or fog have a cooling influence, rupturewort will grow in full sun.

Soil should be well-prepared with compost and organic phosphorus. Add oyster shell in acidic soils.

Rupturewort needs irrigation at least once a week in the heat of the summer. New plantings will require even more frequent irrigation.

Provide an organic mulch rich in nutrients when first planting starts of *Herniaria glabra.* It will root as it spreads, so the better the mulch, the healthier the growth.

BLOOM

A few very tiny white flowers open in late spring, but *Herniaria glabra* blooms so little that the change may not be noticed.

SEASONAL INTEREST

When it is vigorous where it is growing, *Herniaria glabra* is an attractive plant year-round. In cold winters there may be a subtle color change in the leaves to bronze-red, then in spring the color of the foliage reverts to bright-green with the new growth.

COMPANION PLANTS AND LANDSCAPE USE

This low groundcover may be the perfect place to add a container of spring-flowering bulbs. Or in fall, an attractive ornamental grass in a container may be moved in as a focal point.

Herniaria glabra may also be used as a trailing plant over a wall, with *Campanula poscharskyana* or *Lamium maculatum* 'Album' or 'Roseum' as companions. All will do well with some morning sun.

Young plants or plugs may be planted twelve inches apart for a quickly spreading small-scale groundcover.

Herniaria glabra is a tough evergreen herb to use between stepping stones, even where there is considerable foot traffic. A little trimming may be necessary to keep the *Herniaria glabra* from covering stones.

A large pot with a specimen plant may be even more attractive with a bit of *Herniaria glabra* trailing over the edge of the pot.

Bulbs make good companions for this groundcover. If the foliage of the bulbs affects the foliage of the *Herniaria*, it will recover quickly as the bulbs fade. Choose bulbs with smaller or finer foliage such as the species *Narcissus* and *Crocus*.

PROPAGATION

Herniaria glabra roots quickly as it creeps along the ground. Divisions are easy in any season. Remove a rooted section for replanting. Or use layering techniques to develop a rooted section. A small container of compost and soil placed under a trailing stem will provide the rooting medium. Secure the stem to the soil surface with a small rock or landscape staple. Once rooting has occurred, this division may be removed and planted.

Vegetative propagation of *Herniaria* is also possible during the growing season, and cuttings will root easily.

MAINTENANCE

VERY, VERY EASY! No maintenance is needed. Because it grows as a tight mat, it is too difficult to renew mulch. Start out with good soil and the planting of *Herniaria glabra* should do well for many years.

Iris unguicularis

IRIS

Iris unguicularis
(winter iris)

This particular iris may be used as a single specimen for a small-scale groundcover, or massed for a larger area. For detailed information, see "Deer in My Garden, Vol. 1".

Lamiastrum galeobdolon

Lamium galeobdolon (Lamiastrum galeobdolon)
(dead nettle, yellow archangel)

An evergreen native from western Europe to Iran, *Lamiastrum galeobdolon* is classified in the *Lamium* genus. Its flowers are very similar in structure to other *Lamiums*, but its growth habit is quite different.

DESCRIPTION

Long vining stems to two feet grow vigorously, with a new layer of growth added each year to the old. Silver and green leaves are two inches in length and one inch in width. The effect of this mass of evergreen foliage under a shade tree, to fifteen inches in height, is bold and beautiful.

Lamiastrum has attractive yellow flowers that open in early spring in my garden, one of the first of perennials to bloom.

CULTURAL REQUIREMENTS

Lamiastrum galeobdolon is a good plant in cold climates. It seems to adapt well to a range of temperatures, including my very hot summer temperatures (to 105°F) as long as it is in shade. The desert is probably the only place it would not do well.

Shade to partial shade are the best exposures for yellow archangel. As soon as it reaches sun, this vigorous perennial declines.

For years I tried to establish a groundcover under my alder, but the tree's shallow roots and greed for moisture and nutrients discouraged almost every plant I tried, until *Lamiastrum* (and *Campanula poscharskyana)*.

Soil should be improved with compost, organic rock phosphate, and oyster shell in acidic soils. A good organic mulch, renewed every few years, keeps this plant thriving. I now have the perfect garden condition for *Lamiastrum,* with alder leaves falling into the bed each fall to add to the mulch.

Yellow archangel may be watered deeply once a week in the heat of the summer. However, it will tolerate less frequent watering if well-mulched. Do not overwater. Leaves will wilt slightly if plants have become too dry.

BLOOM

In bloom, *Lamiastrum* is a welcome splash of color in early spring. Soft-yellow flowers may not be bright, but there are so many that the groundcover becomes a focal spot in the landscape. Erect stalks emerge, holding multiple flowers to eighteen inches.

The common name, yellow archangel, is a reference to the blossoming each year near the day dedicated to the Archangel Michael in Great Britain.

Flowering continues for about three weeks, whether or not *Lamiastrum* is deadheaded.

This is an excellent cut flower, the strong stalks holding up well in fresh arrangements.

SEASONAL INTEREST

Lamium maculatum 'Pink Chablis'

Because it is evergreen, *Lamiastrum* is beautiful year-round. In winter, its foliage lies somewhat lower than during the growing season, but it is still an effective mass of silver and green leaves. Early spring brings a color change with bloom, followed by new growth in mid-spring.

COMPANION PLANTS AND LANDSCAPE USE

Because of the vigorous growth of this groundcover, a tree makes a good companion. Though vining by nature, *Lamiastrum galeobdolon* will not climb up the trunk or into the tree. Ornamental shrubs may be more vulnerable to this groundcover climbing into the plant.

Competition with tree or shrub roots for moisture and nutrients is not a problem with this strong groundcover, as long as compost has been spread at planting time, followed by a good organic mulch.

Even in deep shade, yellow archangel is an excellent groundcover. For seasonal interest, place a large container of bulbs in bloom into the groundcover. It may be moved when the bulbs fade. Near the edge of the *Lamiastrum*, try the bulbs *Leucojum aestivum* (summer snowflake) in large clusters.

PROPAGATION

Where the tips of the vining stems touch the ground, roots will form. When this happens, a new shoot develops. This new shoot provides excellent vegetative material for cuttings. Plus, this section may be cut free of the parent stem and dug up as a separate plant.

Divisions of *Lamiastrum galeobdolon* may also be made by digging up a clump of mature plants and separating them.

MAINTENANCE

VERY, VERY EASY! This is the perfect groundcover for shade. It needs no maintenance, not even the removal of faded flowers. The gardener does not even have to weed the area, because *Lamiastrum galeobdolon* is so vigorous that not a single weed grows!

Lamium maculatum 'Album'

Lamium maculatum
(spotted dead nettle)

The cultivars of this evergreen groundcover include variations in color of both leaves and flowers. The common name originates in the fact that this nettle does not sting. All these wonderful evergreens have a historical significance for herbalists. Culpepper suggested them for bruises, burns, splinters, and even the spirit, stating: "it makes the heart merry, drives away melancholy, quickens the spirit".

DESCRIPTION

Lamium maculatum 'Pink Pewter'

Lamium maculatum does not vine, but spreads quickly as a beautiful low evergreen groundcover. Leaves are heart-shaped, one and one-fourth inch in length, and flowers are closr to the foliage. Most *Lamiums* are under ten inches in height, and spread as a single plant to three feet.

Cultivars have distinct differences as follows:

Lamium '**Album**' has dark-green leaves with a slight amount of silver in the center. Flowers are white.

Lamium '**Aureum**' has golden-green foliage with a slight amount of white in the center. Flowers are pale-pink.

Lamium '**Beacon Silver**' has silvery leaves with green edges and pinkish spots on the foliage. Flowers are pink.

Lamium '**Chequers**' has foliage similar to 'Album' and pink flowers.

Lamium '**Orchid Frost**' has silver and green leaves and orchid-pink flowers.

Lamium '**Pink Chablis**' has light silvery-green leaves edged with midgreen, and light-pink flowers.

Lamium '**Pink Pewter**' has slightly ruffled silvery leaves edged with green, and pink flowers.

Lamium '**Roseum**' has green leaves with a light-green center with rosy-pink flowers.

Lamium '**White Nancy**' has pretty white foliage, delicately edged with green. Flowers are white.

CULTURAL REQUIREMENTS

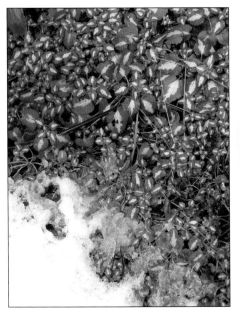

Lamium maculatum 'Roseum'

Similar to *Lamiastrum galeobdolon*, *Lamium maculatum* thrives in many climates, including the cold mountain and intermountain western United States. It is not suitable as a desert plant in lower elevations.

Shade (or partial shade) is the appropriate exposure. The more green in the leaves, the more partial sun the *Lamium* will tolerate. The white leaves of *Lamium* 'White Nancy' are damaged in sun. This cultivar grows quite well in deep shade.

Soil should be enriched with organic compost and rock phosphate. Though tolerant of soil acidity, use some oyster shell in acid soils. Decomposing leaves are a good amendment.

Water carefully. Overwatering will cause lower leaves to yellow. *Lamium maculatum* will tolerate irrigation once a week if soil drainage is good. Irrigation once every two weeks may be sufficient.

Mulch to three-inch depth at planting time. It's difficult to renew the mulch later.

BLOOM

See Description. Flowers form in clusters around the stalk.

Lamium maculatum begins bloom in late spring and most cultivars will continue through the summer. Flower stalks are short, but occasionally long enough for cut flowers. Deadheading will encourage branching and more bloom. Remove just the portion that has flowered as soon as it fades.

Lamium maculatum 'White Nancy'

Unlike *Lamiastrum galeobdolon, Lamium maculatum* is not aggressive. There are many shade to partial-shade perennials that are wonderful companions. All species of *Helleborus* are enhanced with a groundcover of *Lamium* nearby.

This summer, as I write, I am enjoying a hanging basket of annual white *Impatiens* mixed with *Lamium* 'Pink Chablis' on my porch. When fall frost kills the *Impatiens*, I will cut it back and enjoy the *Lamium* all winter. The hanging basket is the only way I can keep the *Impatiens* out of reach of the deer.

Any cultivar of *Lamium maculatum* is beautiful combined with *Asarum caudatum* or *Sarcococca hookerana humilis* either in the garden or in a container. Sweet violets *(Viola odorata)* are another good companion.

Where root competition under ornamental shrubs or trees is a problem in the landscape, *Lamium maculatum* as a groundcover is frequently a good solution. It spreads quickly.

Leucojum aestivum (summer snowflake) are bulbs for partial shade or shade that look very attractive emerging in early spring through a groundcover of *Lamium*. After the bulbs bloom, as the foliage fades it disappears into the groundcover.

Ornamental grasses for shade, *Hakonechloa* (Japanese forest grass), *Miscanthus sinensis* 'Variegata' (variegated maiden grass), *Carex conica* 'Marginata' (variegated dwarf sedge), and *Calamagrostis brachytricha* (fall-blooming reed grass) are even more beautiful when surrounded by *Lamium*. Any combination of these may be used in containers. In my garden, I have a mid-green urn with the golden *Carex flava* (golden sedge) and the dark-green and white *Lamium* 'Album'. This fall I may add some giant snowdrop *(Galanthus elwesii)* for spring bloom next year. *Lamium* is an excellent small-scale groundcover, or an accent for a small garden.

PROPAGATION

Lamium maculatum is easily propagated from vegetative cuttings taken during the growing season. They root quickly.

Divisions may also be made by lifting sections of mature plants during the late fall, winter, or early spring.

MAINTENANCE

VERY, VERY EASY! No maintenance is necessary. Because the plant blooms so freely, removing faded flowers will encourage branching and more flowering. But if this is not done, the plant still looks wonderful all year.

LAVANDULA

Lavandula angustifolia nana 'Alba'
(dwarf white English lavender)

Because it grows low (under one foot) and covers a large area (to three feet), this one cultivar is chosen to be included in this volume as a groundcover, edger, or rock garden specimen. Other lavenders could also serve as large-scale groundcovers. For detailed information see "Deer in My Garden, Vol. 1".

Lysimachia nummularia 'Aurea'

Lysimachia nummularia
(creeping jenny, moneywort)

Lysimachia nummularia is an evergreen European native, growing indigenously in the Caucasus. While three of the taller species within this genus, *Lysimachia punctata*, *Lysimachia ciliata* (including 'Atropurpurea'), and *Lysimachia clethroides* are favorites of the deer in my garden, this attractive groundcover is untouched.

DESCRIPTION

Long stems (to two feet) with rounded leaves grow vigorously, trailing over one another and forming a mat of foliage, usually under four inches in height. The new leaves are very small, lying flat, and along the trailing stems they get progressively larger. The oldest leaves are about one inch. The cultivar 'Aurea' has gold foliage. Sometimes the foliage is more yellow-gold in partial shade and more gold-green in deep shade.

Bright-yellow flowers of *Lysimachia nummularia* open close to the stems in late spring and early summer.

CULTURAL REQUIREMENTS

Lysimachia nummularia will grow in full sun or partial shade. In hottest summer regions, afternoon shade or dappled sunlight under a deciduous tree are the best exposures. 'Aurea' must have lots of shade or the foliage will burn.

BLOOM

Very pretty bright-yellow flowers an inch across open in profusion. The contrast with the green foliage of *Lysimachia nummularia* is quite attractive. Flowering usually lasts for several weeks in late spring and early summer.

SEASONAL INTEREST

Lysimachia nummularia is an attractive evergreen year-round. In bloom, the yellow flowers add a brief seasonal change, then fade into the evergreen foliage.

COMPANION PLANTS AND LANDSCAPE USE

Though its leaves are larger than *Herniaria glabra,* the use and companions for both are very similar. The only difference is that *Lysimachia nummularia* should not be used between stepping stones because it will cover them.

Lysimachia nummularia and *L. n.* 'Aurea' are attractive as evergreen trailing plants over a wall or in a hanging basket.

PROPAGATION

Creeping jenny will root as it trails, and sections may be removed for replanting. Layering is also possible by placing a container of soil mix under a trailing stem, pinning the stem to the surface at a leaf joint, then cutting it from the parent plant once it has rooted.

MAINTENANCE

VERY, VERY EASY! No maintenance is needed for creeping jenny.

Mahonia repens

MAHONIA

A genus that includes deer-resistant evergreen shrubs, *Mahonia* has one species that makes an excellent spreading groundcover.

Mahonia repens (Berberis)
(creeping holly grape)

Native from Northern California into British Columbia, and as far east as the Rocky Mountains, evergreen *Mahonia repens* usually grows as an understory plant in the shade of native trees and shrubs.

DESCRIPTION

Tough, leathery, blue-green leaves do not have the shiny surface of many of the species. In cold winters, the color transitions to bronze with splashes of red and pink. New growth in early spring is light-green. Form of the leaves is similar to holly, and somewhat prickly.

Height is under one foot, and spread to three feet. Creeping holly grape spreads slowly by underground stems.

Bright-yellow flowers are followed by edible blue berries attractive to birds.

CULTURAL REQUIREMENTS

Mahonia repens will tolerate considerable winter cold and summer heat. If gardeners in northern latitudes try to grow this native, they should plant it in a microclimate that offers some winter protection.

Creeping holly grape will grow in full sun, partial shade, or considerable shade. In deep shade, its growth habit may be more leggy. In partial shade, as in sun, growth will be dense and more attractive.

Soil does not need to be rich, but before planting add organic compost and phosphorus, and oyster shell in acidic soils to release nutrients.

Plants should be irrigated for the first two years after planting. If they are well-mulched, they do not need to be irrigated again during the summer. However, they may be irrigated as often as once every two weeks without damage.

Mulches should be of organic materials. Leaves may fall into the groundcover and decompose, adding to the initial mulch.

BLOOM

Flowers are fragrant, bright-yellow, and very attractive, opening in clusters from early to mid-spring. Blue berries form when the flowers fade.

Do not deadhead, or you'll miss the berries, and so will the birds.

SEASONAL INTEREST

Mahonia repens is an excellent evergreen for year-round interest. The changes in foliage color in winter, the bright spring bloom, and the handsome berries are seasonal dynamics that make this plant special.

COMPANION PLANTS AND LANDSCAPE USE

Because of its dense growth, companions should be planted near, but at a distance of five or more feet. If *Mahonia repens* is allowed to overtake a companion, it may be the decline of that plant.

Grown in sun, include *Romneya coulteri* (Matilija poppy) as a nearby companion. Native ornamental grasses such as *Muhlenbergia rigens* (deer grass, basket grass), *Muhlenbergia capillaris* (purple or pink muhley), and *Stipa gigantea* (giant feather grass), are excellent sun-loving accents grown in the proximity of *Mahonia repens*.

Creeping holly grape is a beautiful evergreen for a northern or eastern-facing slope. While it will tolerate the hotter sun of a southern or western-facing slope, it may need irrigation at least once a month in hot-summer climates. In climates with fog or clouds, irrigation in full-sun exposures may be much less.

In the partial shade of native oaks, creeping holly grape is a beautiful large or small-scale evergreen groundcover. Judicious summer irrigation of the *Mahonia* the first two years will not injure the oaks. Keep the *Mahonia* away from the base of the tree, and use drip irrigation to concentrate and minimize watering.

Mahonia repens is not a good evergreen along a walkway because of its prickly leaves.

PROPAGATION

Mahonia repens may be propagated from cuttings taken during the growing season. Plants may also be lifted and divided in late fall or in winter.

Berries will produce seed if birds do not get them first. Plant seed in a loose medium, and barely cover it.

MAINTENANCE

VERY, VERY EASY! No maintenance is required.

Myosotis scorpioides
(forget-me-not)

Forget-me-nots are a classic flower for spring bloom. Most commonly seen is the annual or biennial, *Myosotis sylvatica,* which naturalizes in woodlands or damp semi-shady areas of the garden. *Myosotis scorpioides* is a perennial species.

DESCRIPTION

This semi-evergreen forget-me-not has a different growth habit than the common annual form. It is not as bushy. It sprawls on the ground, its delicate branching stems reaching lengths of two feet. Blue flowers open in late spring and continue into summer.

CULTURAL REQUIREMENTS

Myosotis scorpioides will grow in the coldest regions of the western United States. It adapts to a wide range of winter cold and summer heat as long as its soil and moisture requirements are met.

Perennial forget-me-not does best in partial shade. In deep shade it will not bloom as well, and plants tend to be a bit rangy. The annual forget-me-not seems to thrive in partial shade or deep shade.

Soil should be rich, and very high in humus. Add lots of compost at planting time, and a good supply of organic phosphorus. Gardeners with acidic soils should add oyster shell.

Also called water forget-me-not, *Myosotis scorpioides* loves moisture, and may even be grown as a water plant. However, its color of leaf and flower is not as deep when it is grown in water. Frequent irrigation, as often as every other day in the heat of the summer, will keep this perennial forget-me-not thriving.

A mulch of good rich organic compost is ideal.

BLOOM

Blue flowers with a pink blush near the center are tiny (less than one-fourth of an inch) but open in profusion and are rich with color. Bloom continues for many weeks from spring into early summer, as long as the plant's irrigation needs are met.

SEASONAL INTEREST

Though this forget-me-not is an evergreen perennial in many climates, in winter it is not significant in the landscape. *Myosotis scorpioides* is most beautiful when it is in bloom. Even in a small garden setting it fades from sight after bloom.

COMPANION PLANTS AND LANDSCAPE USE

Since the perennial forget-me-not begins flowering as the annual fades, use it in partial shade to extend the season of forget-me-not bloom.

Myosotis scorpioides adds a delicate touch near the robust dark-green leaves of *Asarum caudatum,* which will also tolerate the moisture the forget-me-not needs.

Ferns are good companions, since they too like moisture.

Use this delicate perennial as a small-scale groundcover near a water feature.

Hanging baskets which are watered frequently offer another landscape use for perennial forget-me-not.

PROPAGATION

Myosotis scorpioides is easily propagated by vegetative cuttings taken during the growing season. There's no hurry in potting it up when rooted, since it loves humid conditions.

MAINTENANCE

EASY! Perennial forget-me-not is semi-evergreen where winters are cold. In my garden I cut it back at the end of winter to encourage fresh new growth, which seems more attractive. If this maintenance is not done, the plant will still do well in the next growing season.

Nepeta x *faassenii* 'Blue Wonder'

NEPETA

Nepeta
(catmint)

Nepetas are wonderful evergreens and evergrays for the rock garden, for slopes, and for groundcovers. Species and cultivars are grouped together here because of their similarity in cultural requirements and landscape use. Distinctions are noted in the following descriptions.

DESCRIPTION

Nepeta reichenbachiana: this catmint is native to Armenia and the Caucasus. Leaves are about one inch in length, light gray-green above and whitish-gray beneath. Flowers are mid-blue with a violet cast. This is the smallest *Nepeta* in my rock garden, with a spread to eighteen inches and a height under one foot.

Nepeta 'Six Hills Giant': Much larger than other species and cultivars of *Nepeta*, 'Six Hills Giant' is true to its name, as tall as three feet and spreading three to four feet or more. Foliage is more gray-green than the other species described in this section, and the flowers are deeper blue, on stalks to eighteen inches.

Note: *Nepeta* 'Six Hills Giant' is described as a separate cultivar here, following its classification in "Hortus Third".

Nepeta x *faassenii*: This hybrid includes several worthy cultivars. 'Walker's Low' has a compact habit, greenish-gray foliage with a two-foot spread, height under one foot, and blue-violet flowers.

'Blue Wonder' and 'Snowflake' have a compact habit of growth with an eighteen-inch to two-foot spread, under one-foot height and greenish-gray foliage. 'Snowflake' has very nice white flowers, and 'Blue Wonder' violet-blue flowers. 'Select Blue' is similar in habit, with dark-blue flowers.

All the *Nepeta* have a mounding habit of growth. As they continue bloom into summer, the center frequently opens and new growth appears.

CULTURAL REQUIREMENTS

All the *Nepeta* described here will grow in very cold and very hot climates. They seem to do equally well in the moderate climates near the coast and in the scorching summer heat of the Sierra Nevada foothills. This is a tough evergray.

Full sun is the best exposure, and this plant will thrive in western or southern exposures, including hot and dry slopes.

Soil should not be rich, but the addition of organic compost and phosphorus is still important. Add oyster shell in acidic soils. Good drainage is essential, especially in winter.

Watering once every two weeks in my clay loam in the heat of the summer has been sufficient irrigation. I have also tested *Nepeta* with no summer irrigation. Without watering, *Nepeta* flowers for a few weeks but it does not continue to bloom.

Mulches may be organic materials, gravel, or even rocks.

BLOOM

Color of bloom is noted under Description above. Flowers are white, shades of blue, and blue-violet. Stalks are spikes with clusters of flowers, very attractive to bees and butterflies. With the initial wave of bloom, flowering stalks cover the foliage.

If the plant begins to open up in the center, it may be cut back to the crown and a new wave of foliage and bloom will follow.

This is a good cut flower for fresh arrangements.

COMPANION PLANTS AND LANDSCAPE USE

All *Nepetas* may be used in the rock garden as single specimen plants. The smaller *Nepeta* work well as edging plants near plants with similar requirements, such as *Lavandula* (lavender), *Santolina* (lavender cotton) or any of the gray-leafed *Thymus*.

Because of the grayish foliage of the *Nepeta,* many of the *Thymus* (thyme) with green foliage are excellent companion plants. While they bloom at the same time, it is the contrasting foliage throughout the year that makes the strongest landscape statement. Irrigation would need to meet the needs of the thyme once every two weeks in the heat of the summer. In this situation, the *Nepeta* would have to have excellent drainage.

Nepeta may be used in a large container allowing for root development. In a container, it should be cut all the way back as the first bloom fades. New growth and more flowers will appear quickly.

Nepeta is also a good low, mounding plant to use with *Iris spuria* since both prefer a drier soil. *Cerastium* (snow-in-summer) is a good companion because its foliage is white or blue-gray in contrast to the gray-green of the *Nepeta.*

Several plants grouped together make an excellent groundcover. Most species will be planted two to three feet apart, but the larger 'Six Hills Giant' may be spaced four to five feet apart.

Because *Nepeta* is cut back to the crown in late winter, *Narcissus* species may be used as companions. Plant clusters or drifts of the bulbs at least two feet away from the center of the *Nepeta*. As the *Nepeta* foliage extends in late spring, it will cover the fading bulb foliage.

A perfect plant for a hot slopes with a western or southern exposure, *Nepeta* joins *Lavandula* (lavender), *Origanum* (oregano), *Rosmarinus* (rosemary), *Santolina* (lavender cotton), *Cotoneaster, Thymus glabrescens* (Loveyanus thyme), and *Teucrium cossonii* ssp. *majoricum* (germander) in solving this difficult landscape challenge. Add a few *Stipa gigantea* as textural accents, and a difficult slope becomes a beautiful focal landscape. Refer to Appendix 3 for a complete list of companions.

PROPAGATION

Nepeta are easily propagated from vegetative cuttings taken from plant material that is not elongating into bloom. Early spring cuttings work well. Cuttings may also be taken from new shoots as soon as the first wave of bloom is fading.

Older clumps may be divided during the winter. Cut back all the stalks and stems to the crown, then cut off a section of the plant for dividing. Divisions do not slip apart easily. They may have to be cut into smaller sections.

MAINTENANCE

Nepeta x *faassenii*

EASY! *Nepeta* looks best if it is cut back to the crown in late winter, removing all stalks and stems. New growth makes a handsome mounding plant in early spring. However, if *Nepeta* has been planted on a difficult slope, without any maintenance it will still look presentable from a distance. Old growth from the previous season will be covered by the new growth.

OENOTHERA

Oenothera tetragona

Oenothera tetragona
(sundrops)

Sundrops is a dynamic small-scale groundcover, edger, or rock garden specimen. For detailed information, see "Deer in My Garden, Vol. 1".

Origanum vulgare nanum

ORIGANUM

Origanum
(oregano)

Species of *Origanum* include several deer-resistant perennial herbs of Europe, the Mediterranean region and central Asia. Some are used for culinary purposes as noted, and a few are strictly ornamental. Most are evergreen. Distinctions between species are noted in description.

DESCRIPTION

Origanum 'Betty Rollins': A beautiful evergreen groundcover, this oregano is a hybrid. It will not survive in the coldest zones. In my garden where the winter temperatures have been as low as 8°F with no snow cover, it shows no winter damage. Dark-green leaves grow thickly on short stems to three inches. In bloom with light-pink flowers, its height is six inches. Though it has some herbal pungency, it is not used for culinary purposes.

Origanum laevigatum: This inedible species spreads as a low evergreen groundcover to three feet or more, with flower stalks that may be as tall as two feet in bloom. It is hardier to winter cold, surviving in the coldest regions of the mountain and intermountain western United States. Leaves are mid-green and airy delicate flowers are mid-pink. 'Hopley's' is a cultivar with darker flowers and some purple in the leaves.

Origanum libanoticum

Origanum libanoticum & *Origanum pulchellum* (**pretty oregano**): Two inedible species adaptable to cold climates, these oregano are not evergreen where temperatures are below freezing cold in winter. They are attractive trailing plants, best used where they can spill over a wall or in a hanging basket because of the flopping flowering habit. Mid-green leaves make an attractive groundcover, and pink flowers in bracts are in abundance on two-foot stems. Based on my observations, the plant I purchased as *O. libanoticum* had larger bracts than *O. pulchellum*.

Origanum sipyleum (**showy pink oregano**): Foliage is blue-green, forming a mound to an eighteen-inch width. In summer, showy sprays of violet-pink flowers open in pale-green bracts. Stalks are one foot to eighteen inches in height. Mass as a groundcover, use as an edger, or grow a single specimen in a sunny rock garden.

Origanum vulgare (**common oregano**): Native to Europe and Asia, evergreen cultivars of *Origanum vulgare* vary considerably in pungency.

All are hardy in very cold zones, including Alaska. If you are using this common oregano for cooking, crush a leaf to decide whether you have a good pungent cultivar.

Origanum vulgare **'Aureum' (gold common oregano)** has golden-green leaves, and purple-pink bracts with tiny, white flowers on short stems. 'Aureum' is compact, under six inches in height and spreading to two feet. This is the best cultivar for semi-shade.

Origanum vulgare nanum **(dwarf common oregano)** is one of my favorite compact evergreen rock garden plants. Its dark-green leaves are slightly smaller than the other cultivars in this species, grouped tightly on short stems under two inches. Purple-pink flowers in bracts bloom on short stalks to four inches.

CULTURAL REQUIREMENTS

Winter hardiness is noted above. Oreganos thrive in summer heat but also do well in more moderate climates.

Full sun is the best exposure, but *Origanum* is tolerant of light shade. The cultivar 'Aureum' should be grown in partial shade in hot-summer areas.

All of the oreganos are undemanding of soil fertility. With a little compost added, oregano grows well even in rocky soil. Add organic phosphorus for good root growth and flowering, and oyster shell in acidic soils.

Deep irrigation once every two to three weeks is sufficient in my clay loam in the foothills of the Sierra Nevada where summer temperatures may reach 105°F. I have *Origanum laevigatum* growing along the edge of my driveway where it gets watered once a month, and it is doing fine. This is a very drought-tolerant perennial.

Origanum will tolerate more frequent watering with no adverse effect. Mulches may be of organic materials, gravel or rocks.

BLOOM

Differences in color of flowers are noted in Description. The structure of the blooming stalk is complex, with small flowers held in bracts. Sometimes the color of the bracts is more dominant than the color of the flowers.

Bloom begins in early summer and continues through the summer for most cultivars. Even as the color of the bloom fades, the flowering structure is still interesting.

All the oreganos make good cut flowers for fresh arrangements, though the dwarf varieties have stalks that are very short. *Origanum laevigatum* and *Origanum sipyleum* are also very nice dried as everlastings.

SEASONAL INTEREST

The evergreen *Origanum* species (see Description) are interesting year-round, their dark-green leaves an accent in the winter garden. Spring brings new growth of foliage and an attractive low mounding habit. Blooms in summer are not bright, but add color and interesting texture above the foliage.

COMPANION PLANTS AND LANDSCAPE USE

Origanum sipyleum

Origanum species are excellent rock garden plants. The two most compact cultivars are *Origanum* 'Betty Rollins' and *Origanum vulgare nanum*. Use these two gems in the rock garden as single specimen accent plants. Several plants placed one foot apart are good small-scale groundcovers or edging plants for a dry edge of the border.

Because of their tolerance for hot conditions, all species will do well with a western or southern exposure, including slopes. Even the two species with bending flower stalks, *Origanum laevigatum* and *Origanum libanoticum,* adapt to a slope with billowing flowers. These two species also do well spilling over a wall or the edges of a large container. See Appendix 3 for a list of companions.

Festuca is a good companion for the compact *Origanum vulgare nanum*. Any of the dwarf blue fescues look wonderful with the dark-green foliage of the oregano. The ornamental grass is complemented by the compact groundcover.

Erigeron karvinskianus (Santa Barbara daisy) is another excellent companion with any of the oreganos. It offers both an echo of color as the white flowers open with a pink tinge, and a contrast of white against purplish-pink as the daisies mature.

Teucrium cossonii ssp. *majoricum* (trailing germander) is a good companion, its gray-green foliage a year-round contrast to the dark-green of the *Origanum*. Flower colors are similar and bloom is synchronized.

PROPAGATION

Division of any of the *Origanum* species is very easy and may be done in almost any season if the foliage on the portion removed is cut back.

Vegetative cuttings taken during the growing season root easily, and offer another way to propagate this carefree perennial.

MAINTENANCE

VERY EASY! Remove flowering stalks when you want the plant to look tidier. I usually leave them until late winter, then cut them back to the crown of the plant with hedge clippers.

PENSTEMON

Penstemon pinifolius

Penstemon hirsutus and *Penstemon pinifolius* are described in detail in "Deer in My Garden, Vol. 1". Of the two, *Penstemon hirsutus* has the lowest growth (six inches) when out of bloom and makes a beautiful small-scale groundcover or evergreen accent plant for the rock garden. It is the very fine leaves of *Penstemon pinifolius* that make it an attractive taller (ten inches out of bloom) evergreen groundcover.

Penstemon fruticosus 'Purple Haze' and *Penstemon gentianoides* were left alone by the deer in my garden, but both were short-lived perennials, surviving only a few years in the rock garden.

Phlox subulata

PHLOX

I have found only one species of *Phlox* that the deer will not eat, *Phlox subulata*. Fortunately it comes in several colors! In fact, "Index Hortensis" lists 42 named cultivars of this wonderful evergreen creeping perennial. I would expect them all to be deer-resistant since the several colors I have tried have been.

Phlox subulata
(moss pink, creeping phlox)

A harbinger of spring, *Phlox subulata* is one of the earliest plants to bloom, following *Potentilla canadensis*.

DESCRIPTION

Very narrow evergreen leaves (to one-half inch) grow densely on foot-long trailing and branching stems. Color varies from mid-green to dark-green. Each plant spreads to two to three feet, and is under six to ten inches in height. In early spring, bright flowers open in abundance.

CULTURAL REQUIREMENTS

Phlox subulata

Phlox subulata does very well in cold climates. *Phlox subulata* is hardy in the coldest regions of the western United States.

Moss pink thrives in full sun, including western and southern slopes, or even spilling over walls where there is reflected heat from a sidewalk or street. Where summers are very hot, and temperatures of 100°F or more linger for days, after-noon shade is preferred.

Soil does not need to be rich, but the addition of organic compost is still the best soil amendment. Also add organic phosphorus, and oyster shell in acidic soils.

Phlox subulata is drought-tolerant as a mature plant. Irrigation once every two to three weeks is sufficient, though more frequent irrigation may keep the foliage more attractive in the heat of the summer. Watch for yellowing foliage when *Phlox subulata* is included in a more frequent-ly irrigated landscape, and reduce the watering if necessary.

BLOOM

Phlox subulata is a very bright spot of color in early spring. Even a sin-gle plant is a dynamic focal spot in the landscape. Whether the flowers are pink, lavender-blue, white, or variations of these colors, a plant in bloom is beautiful.

Each flower is about three-fourths an inch in width, and there are so many that it's difficult to see the foliage. Bloom continues for three to four weeks in spring.

Deadheading by shearing the plant after bloom encourages new foliage growth which will produce even more flowers for the next season.

SEASONAL INTEREST

As an evergreen, *Phlox subulata* is an attractive addition to the garden year-round, especially when it has been maintained by shearing after bloom.

The most dynamic season of interest is in early spring when new growth starts and buds are forming, and continues to a peak when creeping phlox is in bloom.

COMPANION PLANTS AND LANDSCAPE USE

Phlox subulata

One of the best companions for *Phlox subulata* is *Narcissus* (daffodils), all kinds. A drift of *Narcissus* naturalized with creeping phlox is a breathtaking sight.

An attractive companion is the evergray *Potentilla canadensis*. Year-round, the bluish gray-green of the *Potentilla* is a pleasing contrast to the green of the *Phlox subulata*. Also, the fine leaves of moss pink are a good textural contrast to the broader leaves of the *Potentilla canadensis*. A few of the yellow flowers of the *Potentilla* may still be open when *Phlox subulata* steals the show.

Phlox subulata is terrific as a single specimen plant in the rock garden. It is also good small-scale groundcover, or several plants may be planted two feet apart to cover a larger area. It's a great wall plant where it may be allowed to spill over the edge.

Southern and western slopes are challenging to landscape. This is one evergreen perennial that will meet the challenge. Here it joins *Origanum* (oregano), *Cotoneaster*, *Lavandula* (lavender), *Santolina* (lavender cotton), and *Teucrium cossonii* ssp. *majoricum*. See Appendix 3.

Phlox subulata is also a good edging plant for irrigated borders, especially those with dry edges. While its spread is broad, it is not aggressive or invasive.

Several ornamental grasses are effective companions, including *Festuca* species (fescue), *Stipa* species (feather grass), and *Bouteloua gracilis* (blue grama grass).

Phlox subulata may be grown in a container, though it should be cut back right after bloom to encourage new foliage growth.

PROPAGATION

Phlox subulata is easily propagated from vegetative cuttings taken during the growing season. This may be done just as flowering wanes and before shearing, since new growth will already have started.

Divisions may also be made from mature plants by lifting sections in late fall or in winter in mild climates.

MAINTENANCE

Phlox subulata

EASY! While creeping phlox will grow and bloom from year-to-year with no maintenance, its best performance is encouraged by shearing soon after bloom. With hedge clippers, cut back one-half of the plant. Do not trim it again in fall or winter or you will be eliminating flowers for the next season.

Note: *Phlox stolonifera* is an attractive groundcover but has been eaten by the deer every time I tried to grow it in my garden.

Potentilla canadensis

POTENTILLA

A genus that includes groundcover species as well as shrubby species, *Potentilla* does include plants that the deer will eat. Fortunately, the most attractive and least invasive groundcover is deer-resistant.

Potentilla canadensis
(creeping cinquefoil)

A rare form of evergray cinquefoil found from Nova Scotia to Ontario, *Potentilla canadensis* is easily propagated and should be included in more gardens.

DESCRIPTION

Potentilla canadensis has greenish-gray leaves with a bluish cast. Similar to a strawberry leaf, the leaf is compound, in three distinct parts. Each one has an attractive toothed edge. This compound leaf is attached with others to a short stem.

Growth is very low, under three to four inches. Given space, plants will continue to spread though they are neither aggressive or invasive.

Bright-yellow flowers appear in very early spring.

CULTURAL REQUIREMENTS

Potentilla canadensis

This is a good evergray *Potentilla* for gardens with cold winters. It does very well with summer heat.

Full sun is a good exposure. I have also tried it as a small-scale groundcover on a slightly northeastern slope where it thrives despite reduced light in winter. *Potentilla canadensis* will grow in partial shade, in an eastern exposure, or on a slope.

Soil does not need to be rich, but the addition of both organic compost and phosphorus is essential. In acidic soils add oyster shell.

Irrigation once every two to three weeks in the heat of the summer in my clay loam has been sufficient. On a slope, where soil may dry out more quickly, water deeply once every ten to fourteen days.

Apply an organic mulch for the plants to spread into and cover it with gravel to maintain moisture while allowing for drainage.

BLOOM

Bright-yellow flowers one-half inch in diameter open just above the foliage in early spring. The contrast of the bright-yellow against the greenish-gray foliage is very striking. Multiple flowers continue to open in succession for about four weeks.

SEASONAL INTEREST

The attractive evergray foliage of *Potentilla canadensis* is interesting in both shape and color, making this plant a focal point in my rock garden year-round. When the bright-yellow flowers are the first blossoms to open in early spring, this outstanding perennial announces another season of gardening pleasures.

COMPANION PLANTS AND LANDSCAPE USE

Potentilla canadensis (foreground) and *Euphorbia amygdaloides* ssp. *robbiae*

Potentilla canadensis is a strong spreader and should not be planted near small alpines unless rocks confine the *Potentilla*.

All species of *Dianthus* described in this volume are good companions, though their bloom will be much later than the *Potentilla*. Remember that foliage contrasts last longer than the fleeting displays of blooms.

The species of *Thymus* (thyme) with dark-green leaves are excellent companions for foliage contrasts. Allow plenty of space for each plant. Three feet of separation is not too much.

Erigeron karvinskianus (Santa Barbara daisy) is a lovely companion, its pink and white flowers a delicate contrast to the leaves of the creeping cinquefoil.

Many of the spring bulbs, including *Allium moly, Galanthus,* and *Narcissus* (especially the small species) are attractive companions. Though initially planted away from the *Potentilla canadensis*, this groundcover may spread to cover the bulbs. When this happens, the bulbs will come up through the creeping cinquefoil each year with no harm to either.

Though the blue tones of the foliage are similar, the contrasting texture of *Potentilla canadensis* grown near dwarf blue fescue *(Festuca)* is effective. The contrast is in the texture of the leaves.

Potentilla canadensis may be used as a small-scale groundcover, or several may be planted two to three feet apart to cover a larger area. A single plant, spreading to at least two feet, is a terrific accent in the rock garden.

This evergreen creeping cinquefoil also makes a good edging plant, especially for a dry edge of the perennial border. It is one of the few gray-leafed plants that will tolerate more frequent irrigation as long as soil drainage is good, so it has many uses in the landscape.

PROPAGATION

Vegetative propagation done during the growing season, even when the plants are in bloom, is the best way to increase your supply of plants. Reach into the plant to obtain a stem of about two-inch length. Many of the larger leaves will be removed.

As the plant matures, divisions of *Potentilla canadensis* are also possible. Dig into the edge of the plant in late fall or early spring and remove a rooted portion.

MAINTENANCE

Potentilla canadensis

VERY, VERY EASY! No maintenance is required. Faded flowers disappear into the foliage. This plant looks great year after year!

Note: *Potentilla pneumanniana* (*P. verna* 'Nana') has been eaten by the deer in my garden. It is very invasive, and also more demanding of water than *Potentilla canadensis*.

The genus *Pratia* includes species that may be of interest to gardeners in mild (and moist!) climates. I have grown only *Pratia pedunculata,* and the deer do not eat it.

Pratia pedunculata
(Isotoma fluviatilis, Laurentia fluviatilis)
(blue star creeper)

This dainty little evergreen creeper hugs the ground. An Australian plant, it grows best where winter temperatures stay above freezing, though it shows little damage to 15° F.

DESCRIPTION

Tiny bright-green leaves appear to have no stems as they grow very close to the ground. The height is about two inches, and the spread fairly aggressive. This creeper has a strong resemblance to baby's tears, another small groundcover that prefers moist, mild climates. Pretty little pale-blue flowers bloom primarily in spring, but in some climates may bloom for many months.

CULTURAL REQUIREMENTS

This is not a perennial groundcover for cold climates. While it did tolerate temperatures in my garden to 15°F, a winter colder than that ended its show. In warmer microclimates in my region of the Sierra Nevada foothills, *Pratia* may be a good groundcover.

Partial shade is the best exposure. Some bright light is required for good growth and for flowering. Deep shade is not a good exposure. In climates where there are more clouds or fog than sunshine, *Pratia* will tolerate more sun exposure.

Rich soil with plenty of organic compost is essential. Also add organic phosphorus, and oyster shell in acidic soils to release the nutrients.

Frequent irrigation is required, though it does not need to be deep. As long as soil stays moist, and especially if humidity in the area is high, *Pratia* will thrive.

Mulches should be of organic material, though it's not unusual for *Pratia* to spread into a gravel path.

BLOOM

Though small, about one-fourth inch in diameter, *Pratia* flowers are exquisite and quite noticeable. Star-shaped pale-blue flowers bloom in abundance but do not cover the foliage. Flowering may continue for several months when plants are growing in the ideal climate.

SEASONAL INTEREST

In mild climates, *Pratia pedunculata* may be an attractive evergreen year-round. It is fussy about soil and moisture, but if its cultural requirements are met, it spreads readily.

Flowers add a delicate contrasting color with a long period of bloom.

COMPANION PLANTS AND LANDSCAPE USE

Spring-flowering bulbs come up easily through blue star creeper. *Galanthus elwesii* (giant snowdrop) is a lovely small bulb for a companion plant because it will rise above the groundcover. The larger *Leucojum aestivum* (summer snowflake) is also very beautiful in a bed of *Pratia pedunculata.*

In shade gardens, *Pratia* may be the perfect groundcover under shrubs, as it will spread easily in the compost mulch.

Because it is so small and compact, blue star creeper is also a good choice between stepping stones in partial shade.

PROPAGATION

Pratia divides easily at anytime of the year. Best divisions are taken when temperatures are cool in spring and fall.

MAINTENANCE

VERY EASY! As long as it's growing in the right climate and conditions, no maintenance is needed.

Prunella vulgaris

PRUNELLA

A European native that grows indigenously in my gardening region, the western foothills of the Sierra Nevada range, this tough evergreen is a good groundcover.

Prunella vulgaris
(self-heal)

DESCRIPTION

Spreading with foot-long stems, *Prunella vulgaris* has dark-green leaves to two inches long. Growth is very low and branching, forming a mat under three inches in height, with a spread that seems limitless.

Prunella vulgaris blooms with purple flowers in summer.

Prunella grandiflora is a related species that has larger leaves and larger flowers. Cultivars include white ('White Loveliness'), pink ('Pink Loveliness'), a light-purple with touches of white ('Purple Loveliness'), and 'Premium Blue'. Deer may browse on these larger flowers, but rarely eat the foliage.

CULTURAL REQUIREMENTS

Prunella will take a lot of winter cold, thriving in the mountain and intermountain regions of the western United States. The summer heat in my foothill region only seems to make it grow better!

In full sun, *Prunella vulgaris* grows vigorously. It will also adapt to partial shade, where it tends to grow a little taller.

Soil does not need to be rich, but *Prunella* definitely grows better where organic compost and phosphorus have been added. The use of oyster shell to release nutrients in acidic soil is important for most plants, but *Prunella vulgaris* grows well in acid soils even when oyster shell is not used.

Irrigation may be as infrequent as once a month for established plants. Irrigated more frequently, *Prunella vulgaris* responds with lusher growth and sometimes added height, especially of the blooming stalks.

Mulch new plantings with either organic materials or gravel. *Prunella vulgaris* will creep right over any mulch, and root into it.

BLOOM

Prunella vulgaris flowers look like those of *Lamium maculatum*. They are related. Both are in the *Lamiaceae* family, which also includes mint. Clusters of small purple flowers form closely on short stalks to four inches. Blooming begins in June and continues through the summer.

Flowers of *Prunella grandiflora* are taller (to eighteen inches) and a better choice for fresh cut flowers.

Deadheading is a good idea if you don't want this plant to spread by seed. And it will certainly encourage continued bloom.

SEASONAL INTEREST

An evergreen that is attractive year-round, *Prunella vulgaris* often goes unnoticed until it flowers. This is one of my favorite plants because it's so rugged.

Prunella vulgaris

The best use for *Prunella vulgaris* is as a groundcover. Because of its vigorous spreading habit, self-heal may not be the best edging plant for a border of other perennials. It may be invasive.

I have used it along a driveway edge where I needed a tight groundcover that would survive the occasional tire rolling over it. Nearby perennials are vigorous and include *Papaver orientalis* (oriental poppy), *Chrysopsis mariana* (Maryland golden aster), *Helianthus maximilianii* (native perennial sunflower), and *Solidago* (goldenrod). The afternoon shade these taller perennials cast does not inhibit the growth of the *Prunella vulgaris*, and may even benefit the groundcover since it receives very little irrigation water along this dry edge.

Spring-flowering bulbs may be used with *Prunella* as a companion planting. Deer-resistant bulbs include many species and cultivars of *Allium* and *Narcissus*. These larger bulbs will come up easily through a mature stand of *Prunella vulgaris*. The bulb foliage will temporarily overshadow the groundcover, but will not do lasting damage.

Use *Prunella vulgaris* as a groundcover in partial shade, especially where tree roots are competitive for moisture.

Prunella may be used along a path or even between stepping stones. Occasional foot traffic or dogs running on *Prunella* will do little damage. My "lawn" is a tapestry of plants, including one of my favorite evergreen groundcovers, self-heal.

PROPAGATION

Propagation of *Prunella* is very easy from divisions taken in fall, winter, or spring. It recovers quickly from being lifted and divided.

Vegetative propagation is another way to increase the number of plants. Terminal buds should be removed before they elongate into bloom.

If plants are not deadheaded, *Prunella* will also spread from seed, and young volunteers may be lifted and replanted where desired.

MAINTENANCE

VERY EASY! *Prunella* needs no maintenance. Flowers need to be dead-headed only in garden areas where you do not want volunteers. Use this wonderful evergreen groundcover where you won't have to worry about any maintenance, and it can naturalize.

Rosmarinus officinalis 'Lockwood de Forest'

ROSMARINUS

This enduring evergreen grows indigenously near the Mediterranean Sea. All species and cultivars seem to be deer-resistant. While its summer hardiness is well-documented, winter hardiness of rosemary cultivars in varying climates and microclimates is less certain.

Rosmarinus officinalis 'Lockwood de Forest' ('Lockwoodii', 'Forestii', 'Santa Barbara')
(trailing rosemary)

This is one cultivar that has done well in my garden in the coldest winter microclimate (8°F) where other cultivars have not survived. Just a few miles from my garden, in a warmer winter microclimate, *Rosmarinus* 'Prostratus' has done well trailing over a south-facing wall.

DESCRIPTION

Rosmarinus officinalis 'Lockwood de Forest' is an evergreen with a slightly trailing and mounding habit of growth. As it mounds, the trailing branches reach a height of two feet. Narrow bright-green leaves to one-half inch are clustered along strong stems. Spread may reach four to five feet.

Blue flowers open on both new and old growth, blossoming in all seasons in my garden.

CULTURAL REQUIREMENTS

Rosmarinus 'Prostratus'

Trailing rosemary includes several cultivars, but the hardiest to winter cold in my garden has been the cultivar 'Lockwood de Forest'. This tough plant has endured winter temperatures to 8°F with no snow cover to protect it. Other cultivars, including 'Prostratus', have not survived this test.

While it may be tender to winter cold, trailing rosemary, like its upright relatives, will thrive with intense summer heat (to 110°F) as beautifully as it adapts to foggy conditions and even sea spray near the coast.

Full sun is the best exposure, but rosemary will also do well in a half-day of sun, or in bright filtered sunlight on the south side of a deciduous tree.

Rosmarinus officinalis 'Lockwood de Forest' thrives in a western or southern exposure, on a slope, and even with reflected heat from nearby rocks or a wall.

Soil should not be rich, but the addition of compost and organic phosphorus is essential for strong growth. While rosemary adapts to a wide pH range, the addition of oyster shell in acidic soils will stimulate plant uptake of all nutrients. Rosemary does not mind rocky soil.

Irrigation tolerances are broad for a mature rosemary. With good drainage, it will tolerate irrigation once a week in heavy clay soil. It will also survive without summer irrigation in my Sierra Nevada foothill climate. In this climate, the natural rainfall occurs primarily between November and April. The hot, dry summer does not affect the vigor of rosemary. In my garden, I irrigate it deeply once every two to four weeks.

Mulches may be of organic materials, gravel, or rocks. Gardeners in cooler summer climates may want to use rocks for a mulch to increase heat.

BLOOM

Rosmarinus officinalis 'Lockwood de Forest' begins blooming in January and continues for many months. The honeybees love this flower, which looks like a tiny blue snapdragon. Though each flower is barely over one-fourth inch, the flowers clustered along the stems add nice color to the rock garden.

Sprays of trailing rosemary may be cut for fresh flower arrangements. They may also be dried, but it is the foliage, not the flower, that provides everlasting material for arrangements.

Trailing rosemary may be used for cooking at any time of the year.

SEASONAL INTEREST

Trailing rosemary is an evergreen that adds beauty to the garden year-round. Since it begins bloom at a time of the year when neighboring plants show only foliage, the blue flowers attract insects and the gardener.

Blue is an uncommon color in a rock garden of low-irrigation perennials; rosemary will provide the longest show of this color.

COMPANION PLANTS AND LANDSCAPE USE

Good evergreen foliage and an unusually long season of bloom make trailing rosemary an asset for several landscape applications.

Though it spreads to three to four feet, trailing rosemary may be used as a single plant for a small-scale groundcover. A single specimen in the rock garden is a strong accent year-round.

Erigeron karvinskianus is a good companion, its white flowers a nice contrast to the bright-green foliage of the rosemary. Rosemary continues its bloom into the summer months while *Erigeron* is showy. I also like this rosemary with the upright *Teucrium* x *lucidrys* (germander).

Rosmarinus officinalis (both upright and trailing) thrives in many exposures, including the toughest southern and western full-sun conditions, even on a slope. Its companions in these challenging landscape situations include *Origanum* (oregano), *Lavandula* (lavender), *Santolina* (lavender cotton), *Artemisia* (wormwood), *Phlox subulata* (creeping phlox), *Salvia officinalis* (sage), *Teucrium cossonii* ssp. *majoricum* (trailing germander), and *Cotoneaster*. Refer to Appendix 3.

Rosmarinus officinalis 'Lockwood de Forest' may be grown in a container. The larger the pot, the more vigorous the growth will be. Grown in a smaller container, trailing rosemary will need to be replanted every few years with fresh soil mix, pruning it back to twelve inches.

A mass of rosemary as a groundcover is very effective, especially on a slope. One-gallon plants may be planted as close as three feet apart for a good cover within one to two years. This somewhat taller and mounding cultivar of trailing rosemary excludes light, which will reduce weeding problems after the first year.

Trailing rosemary is a good choice for erosion control.

Ornamental grasses with similar cultural requirements are good companions. This includes *Festuca* species (fescue), *Stipa tenuissima* (feather grass) or *Stipa gigantea, Helictotrichon* (blue oat grass), and the native *Muhlenbergia rigens* (basket grass, deer grass) and *Muhlenbergia capillaris* (purple muhley).

PROPAGATION

Propagation is easy from vegetative cuttings taken year-round in my climate. Gardeners with the coldest winters will need to take the cuttings between March and October for best results.

MAINTENANCE

VERY, VERY EASY! No maintenance is needed. Occasionally, a prolonged winter cold spell may kill some foliage, which may be removed.

Rubus calycinoides

Rubus calycinoides
(creeping raspberry)

Native to the Himalayas, *Rubus calycinoides* is an evergreen ornamental bramble that creeps low to the ground.

DESCRIPTION

Each leaf is very attractive, with a rounded and slightly ruffled shape to one and one-half inches in width and length. Leaves are dark-green during most of the growing season but may change to a rust cast in cold winter temperatures. The leaves grow closely together along reddish-brown stems (with tiny barbs), making a thick but low groundcover.

Trailing stems root where they touch mulch. Trailing over a wall, stems may reach a length of three or more feet. A mature planting is usually under ten inches in height. On the ground, *Rubus* continues to spread, rooting as it creeps.

Small white flowers on short stems are barely noticeable above the strong foliage in early summer. Orange berries may appear following flowering.

CULTURAL REQUIREMENTS

Although some garden references classify this perennial as preferring more temperate climates, in my experience it has a broad range of cold tolerance. I have used it on landscapes at 3500-foot elevation where it thrives, and shows no winter damage after snows or in cold temperatures to 8°F with no snow cover.

The summer heat and low humidity in my Sierra Nevada foothill climate do not affect the vigorous growth of *Rubus calycinoides*.

Creeping raspberry prefers partial shade in hot-summer areas. It will even do well in fairly deep shade. In climates where there are clouds or fog in summer, *Rubus* will tolerate more sun.

Soil should be fertile, but does not need to be prepared deeply. Most of the root growth of *Rubus* will be in the top six inches of soil. Add lots of organic compost and phosphorus, with oyster shell in acidic soils.

Irrigate once a week for optimal growth. With less frequent irrigation, or where tree roots are competitive for moisture and nutrients, *Rubus* will still grow well but will not be as lush.

Mulch with organic materials such as decomposing leaves or straw, or compost.

BLOOM

Flowers look like strawberry flowers, only much smaller. Each white blossom is one-half inch or less, and barely noticeable on short stalks held slightly above the foliage. Orange berries are attractive, but not bright. Bloom is very short, only a few weeks in early summer.

SEASONAL INTEREST

Rubus calycinoides is an outstanding evergreen groundcover year-round, especially for partial shade. It makes a thick groundcover that will exclude most weeds.

In cold temperatures, the dark-green foliage has an attractive bronze cast.

COMPANION PLANTS AND LANDSCAPE USE

Rubus calycinoides

Creeping raspberry is a vigorous groundcover that may not be suitable for a small garden, unless it is grown in a container. In a tall container it can trail beautifully over the edges, and will be the perfect accent plant for a semi-shade garden.

On a larger scale, *Rubus calycinoides* is very attractive trailing behind and over a wall.

Several plants massed on two to three-foot centers will cover an area within one to two years. Accent plants in containers (ornamental grasses or bulbs) may be placed within the groundcover to add a focal point.

Plants with similar cultural requirements may be grown nearby as companions. A planting of one of the *Lamium* cultivars provides a beautiful contrast in foliage year-round. The *Lamium* should be planted three to four feet from the *Rubus*.

Strong ornamental shrubs such as *Choisya ternata* (Mexican orange) and *Lonicera nitida* (box honeysuckle) are attractive with a groundcover of *Rubus calycinoides* at their base.

Spring-flowering bulbs will grow through a thick groundcover of *Rubus calycinoides*. Use only large bulbs such as *Leucojum aestivum*.

PROPAGATION

Layering is the fastest way to obtain more plants of *Rubus*. It is natural for this plant to root at the leaf axils as it creeps along the mulch. This may be encouraged by using landscape staples to pin the stem to the ground. Remove this section once it has rooted.

Rubus calycinoides may also be propagated with vegetative cuttings taken March through November in mild climates, and in the summer in any growing climate.

MAINTENANCE

VERY, VERY EASY! No maintenance is necessary.

SALVIA

Salvia officinalis 'Berggarten'

Salvia officinalis
(common sage)

Salvia officinalis includes four cultivars that are excellent as taller groundcovers and edgers: *Salvia officinalis*, *Salvia officinalis* 'Nana', *Salvia officinalis* 'Berggarten', and *Salvia officinalis* 'Purpurascens'.

For detailed information, refer to "Deer in My Garden, Vol. 1".

SANTOLINA

Santolina

Santolina
(lavendar cotton)

All species and cultivars of *Santolina* are very effective as taller groundcovers and edgers.

For detailed information, refer to "Deer in My Garden, Vol. 1".

Sarcococca hookerana humilis

SARCOCOCCA

This genus includes only a few species of evergreen shrubs, native to western China, the Himalayas, and southeast Asia. These beautiful evergreens for shade and partial shade are among my favorite deer-resistant plants. The only one that is a low groundcover is included here.

Sarcococca hookerana humilis
(creeping sweet vanilla plant, sweet box)

DESCRIPTION

Dark-green leaves are more narrow and longer than those of the shrub species of *Sarcococca*. Each mature pointed leaf is three-fourths inch at the center, and tapered on each end. The effect of these narrow leaves growing densely on loosely upright stems is unusual and attractive.

Evergreen *Sarcococca* has a mounding habit of growth, under one foot in height, and spreading slowly to three feet or more. White flowers are significant in fragrance, but not in color impact.

CULTURAL REQUIREMENTS

Sarcococca hookerana humilis will grow in cold climates in the western United States, but not in Alaska.

The best exposure is partial shade. While it will also grow well in full shade, bloom will not be as heavy.

Soil should be fertile, with the addition of organic compost and phosphorus. Gardeners with acidic soils should add oyster shell.

Creeping sweet vanilla plant will grow in soils where there is competition for nutrients and moisture from nearby shrubs or trees.

This is not a high-irrigation groundcover, but it will tolerate watering once a week. Watering may be less frequent or even more frequent, and *Sarcococca hookerana humilis* will thrive.

Mulches should be of organic materials, and renewed each year, especially where there is root competition.

BLOOM

Tiny, fragrant white flowers open in late winter, followed by black berries. This is an excellent plant to use for fresh arrangements. Stems cut when the flowers first open will hold the fragrance inside your home.

The foliage used in fresh arrangements, even when out of bloom, is very attractive.

SEASONAL INTEREST

Sarcococca hookerana humilis is a beautiful evergreen for year-round interest. Fragrance in late winter is special, and the black berries that follow the insignificant white flowers extend the flowering season.

COMPANION PLANTS AND LANDSCAPE USE

Use creeping sweet vanilla plant as an evergreen groundcover on a small or large scale in partial shade.

It is also an excellent edging plant along a walkway or path where its late-winter fragrance will be noted by passersby. Grow it near a bench!

As a container plant, this *Sarcococca* is very attractive.

Companions include those plants that prefer some shade: *Asarum caudatum* (ginger), *Lamium maculatum* cultivars, *Veronica liwanensis,* and variegated ornamental grasses (*Carex, Molinia,* and *Hakonechloa).*

Used as a companion groundcover under *Choisya ternata* (Mexican orange), *Sarcococca hookerana humilis* is an interesting contrast in leaf and plant form. This is an effective groundcover under a deciduous tree, even one with shallow roots.

A small area of the *Sarcococca* is a good accent in a garden of any size.

Bulbs will not come up through the *Sarcococca,* but they may be planted nearby as companions. *Leucojum aestivum* (summer snowflake) is the deer-resistant bulb most tolerant of shade.

PROPAGATION

Vegetative cuttings of *Sarcococca hookerana humilis* root easily. Take these cuttings from April through October.

Divisions may also be made by lifting a portion of the plant during the late fall, or winter in mild climates. Carefully pull apart the lifted portion to obtain as many rooted divisions as possible.

MAINTENANCE

VERY, VERY EASY! No maintenance is required. Renew the mulch every year or every few years.

SOLIDAGO

Solidago 'Golden Baby'
(dwarf goldenrod)

Solidago 'Golden Baby' is a good compact plant for a small-scale groundcover, or as an edging plant. For details, see "Deer in My Garden, Vol. 1".

Spiraea japonica 'Alpina'

SPIRAEA

A genus within which several species are deer-resistant, *Spiraea* includes many small shrubs. The one that is the best as a low groundcover, *Spiraea japonica* 'Alpina', is uncommon, but a very worthy deciduous groundcover, edger, or rock garden specimen.

Spiraea japonica 'Alpina' ('Nana')
(alpine spirea)

I have had *Spiraea japonica* 'Alpina' in my garden for several years. One of my specimens is almost half the size of the other though they are the same age and had the same label.

DESCRIPTION

Spiraea 'Alpina' is a low-growing deciduous shrub. This size of shrub is commonly called a subshrub. A mature specimen is eighteen to twenty-four inches in height and three to five feet in spread.

Habit is shrubby and mounding, with multiple branches. Leaves range in size from one-half inch to more than one inch. Light-pink flowers open in early summer.

CULTURAL REQUIREMENTS

This hardy *Spiraea* will grow in cold regions, including the coldest areas in the mountain and intermountain western United States.

Spiraea japonica 'Alpina' needs lots of sun to grow and bloom well. Full sun is an excellent exposure. In hot-summer areas, this tough plant performs beautifully with a half-day of morning sun. It will also endure morning shade followed by hot afternoon sun. Shade in winter is not a problem because this subshrub is deciduous.

Soil should be fertile, but does not need to be rich. Because this is a plant that will remain where planted for many years (unless, of course, the gardener decides it must be moved), good soil preparation in the beginning is essential. Add at least one-third organic compost to two-thirds native soil, plus organic phosphorus, and oystershell in acidic soils.

Irrigation once a week in clay loam in the heat of the summer is best, though *Spiraea* will certainly survive with less, especially if it is mulched. Growing in afternoon shade, my plants receive water every ten to fourteen days in summer. Gardeners with sandy soil should add a compost that retains moisture. In areas with fog or clouds in summer, *Spiraea* 'Alpina' is drought-tolerant.

Mulches should be of organic materials to add nutrients and retain moisture. Renew them every year, if possible.

BLOOM

Tiny, single light-pink flowers form in clusters at the end of branches. The effect is a mound covered in flowers when *Spiraea* is in bloom in early summer. Even after the color fades, the form of the flower cluster adds an interesting texture to the plant as it goes into the seed stage.

The name *Spiraea* is from the Greek *speiraira,* a plant used in garlands. Flowers may be used for fresh cut arrangements by removing a section of the branches. Leave enough of the lower branch for it to regrow.

SEASONAL INTEREST

This plant is interesting year-round. At its height when it is in bloom with light-pink flowers covering the mid-green foliage, *Spiraea japonica* 'Alpina' is a focal plant in my garden in early summer.

Seedheads are light-brown and follow the form of the flower in clusters. They add an interesting texture for the remainder of the summer. In fall, there is a subtle but distinct color change in the leaves to gold and rust-brown.

Even in winter, the delicate bare branches add attractive texture and form to the landscape. When snow is held by the branches, *Spiraea japonica* 'Alpina' is once again a focal plant in my garden.

COMPANION PLANTS AND LANDSCAPE USE

There are many uses for this wonderful plant! For weed suppression, alpine spirea is an effective plant to mass on a slope, a mound, and even a flat area.

A single specimen is very attractive in a container, in the rock garden, behind a retaining wall, or as an edging plant near taller perennials.

Using it as an edging plant, allow enough space for a four-foot spread. Each plant must have sufficient space so that its attractive form will not be overshadowed by taller or more aggressive plants.

There are many companion plants for *Spiraea japonica* 'Alpina'. If the *Spiraea* is used in full sun, *Cerastium* species (snow-in-summer) make good companions. In afternoon shade, the green-leafed species of *Thymus* (thyme) are beautiful evergreens to grow near the *Spiraea*.

Erigeron karvinskianus (Santa Barbara daisy) is a terrific companion in sun or light shade, since it continues flowering when the color of *Spiraea* 'Alpina' fades. In early summer, when the two are in bloom together, there is a subtle color echo of pink.

PROPAGATION

Vegetative propagation should be done in early spring or after bloom in late summer. Cuttings root easily.

MAINTENANCE

VERY EASY! Very little maintenance is needed. Especially for older plants, renewing the mulch with some good compost each year will add nutrients to the soil to maintain vigorous growth and bloom. In some years, I use hedge clippers in late winter to prune lightly. This removes seedheads and encourages growth for more flowering the coming season.

Stachys byzantina

STACHYS

Stachys byzantina (S. lanata, S. olympica)
(woolly betony, lamb's ears, lamb's tongue)

Stachys is a groundcover that seems to delight young and old alike. One day my grandson Marcus lay down in a big bed of *Stachys*, his smile showing how good it felt. I wish I had had my camera.

DESCRIPTION

Very soft, felty leaves grow densely to form a mat of evergray foliage. The species has light-gray foliage and blooms with stalks to two and one-half feet. Flowers are not colorful, although their form is interesting.

The cultivar 'Silver Carpet' has gray-white foliage with a blue tone, and does not bloom.

Leaves are four to six inches in length, clustered in open rosettes. Spread is by surface stolons, and roots are shallow. *Stachys* is a vigorous spreader, and may even be considered invasive by some gardeners. Its dense growth excludes most weeds.

CULTURAL REQUIREMENTS

Stachys is a hardy plant native to the Caucasus Mountains and Iran. It will grow in the coldest regions of the mountain and intermountain western United States. It also endures summer heat and fog.

Full sun is only one of many possible exposures for this tough groundcover. It will grow in full morning shade with hot afternoon sun (a western exposure), in the partial shade of deciduous trees, and in morning sun with afternoon shade.

I have grown *Stachys* at the base of a Ponderosa pine and under the native oaks with no summer irrigation. The semi-shade, dry conditions and infertile soil challenged *Stachys,* but it held on and spread slowly year after year.

Soil should not be rich, but add a little organic compost and phosphorus. Use oystershell in acidic soils as an amendment to release nutrients. Soil preparation does not need to be deep; ten inches is sufficient.

Stachys will grow in rocky or gravelly soil, and does not mind the competition for water or nutrients from nearby trees or ornamental shrubs.

Drainage must be good. *Stachys* is a very low-irrigation perennial groundcover. In my sunny rock garden, in rocky clay soil with a little bit of compost added, *Stachys* is watered once every two weeks. It will tolerate more frequent irrigation in full sun. In partial shade it should be watered less frequently.

Watch for yellowing foliage. This is a sure sign of overwatering.

Mulches should be of small gravel or rocks over a very light layer of compost. Do not renew the mulch of compost for established ground-covers.

BLOOM

Stachys 'Silver Carpet' is a cultivar that does not bloom.

The species blooms with clusters of flowers that look like *Prunella, Lamium,* and *Lamiastrum,* to which it is related. Small, pink flowers are clustered within the flowering structure of the gray stalk. It also has felty leaves below the flower clusters, echoing the form and color of the base leaves.

Flower stalks are an interesting addition to fresh cut flower arrangements.

Deadhead the blooming species by removing the stalks at the base to maintain the attractiveness of the groundcover.

COMPANION PLANTS AND LANDSCAPE USE

Stachys byzantina

Because it is a vigorous groundcover, it must be combined with other plants very carefully. In my rock garden, I am using larger rocks buried ten inches deep into the soil to restrain the *Stachys.* It still tries to climb over the rocks.

Growth may be maintained in a specific area by using the vinyl equivalent of bender board.

The best landscape situation in which to use this plant is where you need a groundcover to cover a large area quickly. Plants may be planted two feet apart, and will fill the area within one year.

Used at the base of ornamental shrubs and small trees, *Stachys* is a useful groundcover. If it spreads into unwanted areas it is easily dug out to restrain the growth each year.

A single plant is an interesting accent in a container. The soil mix will need to be renewed at least every other year. Prune the roots and the top growth when you are repotting.

I enjoy a small area of *Stachys* 'Silver Carpet' where it spills over the edge of my stone walkway. Similarly, it may be used at the top of a rock wall, where it will spill over without covering the beautiful stones.

Stachys joins the list of perennials that will tolerate a western exposure with hot afternoon sun. See Appendix 3. My favorite companion plant is the upright rosemary *(Rosmarinus officinalis)*. Its dark-green foliage has a fine texture played against the larger soft-gray foliage of the *Stachys*.

The green lavender cotton *(Santolina virens)* and the upright germander *(Teucrium x lucidrys)* are also beautiful companions.

PROPAGATION

Division is the easiest way to propagate *Stachys*. Rosettes of leaves form as the stolons spread, and quickly grow roots. Remove only those portions that show roots. This is best done during the cooler months in spring and fall. Gardeners in mild-winter areas may also do this division in winter.

MAINTENANCE

Stachys 'Silver Carpet'

VERY, VERY EASY! No maintenance is required for *Stachys* 'Silver Carpet' unless you are trying to restrain its growth. The species, *Stachys byzantina,* looks best if flower stalks are removed at the base when they begin to collapse after bloom fades.

Tanacetum densum ssp. *amani*

TANACETUM

The genus *Tanacetum* includes feverfew, a wonderful deer-resistant perennial detailed in "Deer in My Garden, Vol. 1". It also includes a xeriphitic groundcover native to Turkey, *Tanacetum densum* ssp. *amani*.

Tanacetum densum ssp. *amani* (*T. d.* 'Amanum')
(tansy)

This beautiful evergray should be included in more low-irrigation gardens. While uncommon, it is very easy to propagate and grow.

DESCRIPTION

Silvery-white leaves are feathery in appearance, forming loose rosettes on silvery-white stems. Their delicate structure is an intriguing contrast to the strength of this evergray perennial.

Growth is slow, with a spread to three or four feet, and a height of under six inches before bloom (ten to twelve inches in bloom).

Similar to *Cerastium Biebersteinii*, the overall appearance of *Tanacetum densum* ssp. *amani* is very white.

Flowering begins in early summer and continues for several weeks. Flower stalks are silvery-white, with yellow flowers.

CULTURAL REQUIREMENTS

This dwarf tansy is a groundcover that will take considerable heat and winter cold. It may not be as attractive in humid climates as it is in arid climates.

Full sun is the only exposure in which *Tanacetum densum* ssp. *amani* will thrive. The more sun and heat the better. Plant it on a southern or western slope.

Soil should not be rich, but the addition of organic compost and phosphorus in clay or sandy soils will add nutrients and aeration. Gardeners with acidic soils should also add oystershell. *Tanacetum densum* ssp. *amani* will grow in rocky soil.

Do not overwater. This is a good groundcover or edging plant for dry areas. The plant is most attractive when it is watered once every three to four weeks. It will tolerate more frequent irrigation if the soil drains well.

Mulches should not be of organic materials. Use small rocks or gravel.

BLOOM

Tanacetum densum ssp. *amani* is attractive in bloom, when white branching stalks elongate with tiny yellow balls clustered at the top.

Flower stalks are beautiful in cut flower arrangements, and good for everlastings.

Deadheading will not increase or lengthen bloom. The stalks are attractive even after the yellow flowers fade. Remove them only when you want to the plant to look neater.

SEASONAL INTEREST

This is an evergray groundcover with white foliage that is beautiful all year. It is also attractive in bloom, though the flowers do not add a strong color to the landscape.

COMPANION PLANTS AND LANDSCAPE USE

Tanacetum densum ssp. *amani* is a beautiful plant for a xeriphitic garden, its white foliage contrasting with grays, blue-grays, and every shade of green.

Use this plant as a single specimen, or as a small or large-scale groundcover. Its tolerance of heat and sun, western and southern slopes, and need for low-irrigation conditions limit its companions to those plants with similar requirements. One of my favorite companions is the dark-green *Rosmarinus officinalis* (upright rosemary). Refer to Appendix 3 for a complete list of suitable companions.

Tanacetum densum ssp. *amani* is very pretty at the edge of a walkway or path. Place it where you will enjoy its lacy foliage close-up.

This is also a lovely plant in a container because it is slow to spread. Do not overwater. Yellowing leaves will be the first sign of over-irrigation.

PROPAGATION

Vegetative cuttings taken during the growing season root easily. Move them to drier conditions as soon as they have rooted, or you may lose them.

MAINTENANCE

VERY EASY! When faded flower stalks appear unattractive, cut them back at the base. No winter maintenance is required.

Teucrium x *lucidrys*

TEUCRIUM

Teucrium is a genus that includes very attractive evergreen and evergray groundcover species. These Mediterranean natives are strong perennials. I have separated them in this volume because their individual descriptions, needs, and uses are distinctly different.

Teucrium cossonii ssp. majoricum
(T. cussonii majoricum, T. majoricum)
(trailing germander)

An evergray germander, *Teucrium cossonii* ssp. *majoricum* is not hardy in very cold climates.

DESCRIPTION

Teucrium cossonii has narrow, gray-green leaves to one inch in length. Trailing and branching stems are somewhat fragile, but this evergray plant is a very tough groundcover. Height of a mature plant is under eight inches, and width may be to three feet, given space and good soil in which to spread.

Growth habit is both trailing and mounding. A single plant spreads at the crown, but the trailing stems may also root.

The primary plant has deep roots, and the trailing stems have more shallow roots.

Rosy-purple flowers begin blooming in early summer and continue into fall.

CULTURAL REQUIREMENTS

Teucrium cossonii ssp. *majoricum*

This evergray germander is not hardy in very cold winter climates. However, it does quite well in my garden, a cold microclimate where winter temperatures dip to 8° F with no snow cover for protection.

Teucrium cossonii ssp. *majoricum* thrives in the summer heat of the Sierra Nevada foothills.

Full sun is the best exposure. In one landscape I used it in a planter in full sun. It has draped over the north wall of the planter with no winter damage.

Good drainage is absolutely necessary in all seasons, but especially in winter if gardeners have heavy clay soils. Trailing germander does well in rocky or gravelly soils.

Either clay or sandy soils should be amended with organic compost. Avoid adding compost that is high in nitrogen. Add organic phosphorus for good root growth and flowering, and oyster shell in acidic soils to release nutrients.

Southern and western exposures, including slopes, are good exposures for this gray-leafed germander. Reflected heat from a walk, driveway, or rocks will not injure it.

Teucrium cossonii ssp. *majoricum* is a low-irrigation groundcover that does not do well when it is overwatered. Cold, wet soils in winter may kill it. Prepare soil so that it has good drainage. Water a mature plant deeply once every ten to fourteen days, or less, in the heat of the summer. Overwatering may cause die-back.

Mulches should be gravel or small rocks. A thin layer of compost may be spread as a mulch, but it is better to incorporate it into the root zone at planting time.

BLOOM

Teucrium cossonii ssp. *majoricum* is a striking groundcover when it is in full bloom. Rosy-purple flowers are clustered on short stems, opening just above the foliage. When the first few flowers are opening, it is awash with color over the gray background.

Trailing germander blooms with a few flowers opening in late spring, then quickly emerges into full bloom in early summer, holding the color for several weeks. Strong bloom continues through the summer and into fall if faded flowers are removed. If no deadheading is done, a few flowers will still open throughout the summer and into fall. Bees love this flower!

SEASONAL INTEREST

Although it is evergray, trailing germander is not a striking plant in winter, but it is still attractive in the landscape. As growth begins in very early spring, it gains strength. In bloom it is outstanding!

COMPANION PLANTS AND LANDSCAPE USE

Trailing germander is a strong spreader, but not aggressive or invasive. It may be used to cover large areas, spacing one-gallon plants two to three feet apart for coverage within one year. It may also be used as a small-scale groundcover with a single plant.

Teucrium cossonii ssp. *majoricum* is one of the most beautiful perennial groundcovers to use behind a south or west-facing wall. It is also outstanding on a slope. Companions include *Salvia officinalis* 'Berggarten' (sage), *Stachys* (lamb's ears), *Santolina* (lavender cotton), *Lavandula* (lavender), *Artemisia* 'Powis Castle', and *Rosmarinus* (rosemary), *Cerastium* (snow-in-summer), and gray-leafed *Thymus* (thyme). Refer to Appendix 3.

Erigeron karvinskianus (Santa Barbara daisy) is also a nice companion because the two are in bloom at the same time. The pink of the *Erigeron* as the flowers open is a subtle color echo of the germander blossoms.

Phlox subulata (creeping phlox) blooms earlier, but its bright-green foliage is a striking year-round contrast to the gray-green of the germander.

Use trailing germander in a large container in full sun. It will need to be repotted after two or three years. Depending on the size of the container, water every other day in the heat of the summer, or even less frequently.

PROPAGATION

Vegetative propagation is easy from cuttings taken in spring. Once trailing germander begins to form buds for bloom, it's harder to find good cutting material. Look into the plant for new growth and gently squeeze the terminal bud. If it feels hard, there is probably a flower already developing. Try to find a cutting that feels soft.

Plants may also be divided during the winter. This method of propagating *Teucrium cossonii* ssp. *majoricum* usually requires lifting large sections of the plant.

MAINTENANCE

EASY! As blooms fade, remove them several at a time with hedge shears or grass clippers. This will encourage more branching and bud formation, extending the bloom well into fall.

If you have not cut back the plants following bloom, cut them back a few inches in late winter.

Teucrium polium (T. Polium)

Teucrium polium is unusual, an evergray germander that is distinctly different from any of the other *Teucriums* described.

DESCRIPTION

Teucrium polium

The foliage is silver-white with a blue cast, and is fuzzy. Flowers are chartreuse and are similar in structure to the other *Teucriums*. *Teucrium polium* spreads slowly to eighteen inches. Height is under three inches out of bloom, and six inches in bloom. This is a very compact plant for the rock garden.

CULTURAL REQUIREMENTS

See *Teucrium cossonii* ssp. *majoricum.*

Teucrium polium is even fussier than *Teucrium cossonii* about drainage. It must be planted in full sun year-round. Watering every three weeks or less is ideal.

Do not mulch with any organic materials. A mulch of gravel or small rocks is appropriate.

BLOOM

Teucrium polium blooms in midsummer with clusters of chartreuse flowers on fuzzy silver-white stalks to six inches.

Flowers resemble the other germanders in structure. They are interesting cut flowers.

SEASONAL INTEREST

Teucrium polium is an unusual evergray perennial year-round. The silver-white and soft appearance of this small plant are very attractive.

COMPANION PLANTS AND LANDSCAPE USE

Because it is so low in its irrigation requirements, *Teucrium polium* has a limited number of suitable companions. *Antennaria dioica* (pussy toes) is one of my favorite xeriphitic companions. Another is *Achillea kellereri*, its leaves a similar color, but a very different texture and form.

Teucrium polium is a good small-scale groundcover. It is best as a specimen plant in the rock garden with a western or southern exposure, allowing the best drainage and the most sun and heat.

Use rocks nearby to reflect heat, but do not allow them to cast any shadows. The silver-white foliage against a dark rock highlights this plant, creating a year-round focal point in the rock garden.

Teucrium polium is not a good container plant unless very careful attention is paid to the soil mix (perfect drainage!), and the irrigation practices.

PROPAGATION

Propagation is not difficult as long as cuttings are removed from high humidity as soon as they begin to root. Take vegetative cuttings in spring, before flowering buds form.

MAINTENANCE

EASY! Remove faded flowers right after bloom by cutting the stalks back to the crown.

Teucrium x *lucidrys*

Teucrium x *lucidrys* is a species that includes the upright germander, an excellent groundcover with an eighteen-inch height in bloom. See "Deer in My Garden, Vol. 1" for details. *Teucrium* x *lucidrys* also includes the cultivar 'Prostratum', one of my favorite evergreen groundcovers.

Teucrium x *lucidrys* 'Prostratum' (*Teucrium* x *chamaedrys* 'Compactum')
(prostrate germander)

DESCRIPTION

Dark-green leaves grow densely on three-inch stems. Each leaf is one-half inch in diameter, and rounded with serrated edges. Very attractive! In bloom, stems elongate to four to six inches. Clusters of flowers resemble *Lamium, Prunella,* and *Stachys* in miniature. They all belong to the family *Lamiaceae,* which includes mint.

Spread is by stolons, and very strong, though not invasive. A single plant has a spread of about three feet.

CULTURAL REQUIREMENTS

Teucrium x *lucidrys* 'Prostratum'

Teucrium x *lucidrys* is a species that will tolerate a broad range of cold and heat, including in the coldest winter regions of the mountain and intermountain western United States.

This green-leafed germander, 'Prostratum', will grow in full sun or partial shade. Morning sun with afternoon shade is a good exposure, or light shade under a deciduous tree. Western or southern exposures are also tolerated if there is regular irrigation once every two weeks in the heat of the summer.

Enrich the soil with organic compost and phosphorus. Use oyster-shell in acidic soils. Good drainage is important in all seasons. *Teucrium* x *lucidrys* 'Prostratum' grows well in rocky or gravelly soil. Roots are not deep. Concentrate your amendments in the upper foot of native soil.

In my rock garden, prostrate germander thrives in full sun on the eastern slope of a mounded area. It is irrigated once every two weeks in the heat of the summer. I have also planted it in a similar exposure where a mature plant was watered once every three weeks, and it did very well.

Teucrium x *lucidrys* 'Prostratum' will tolerate irrigation once a week, even in clay soils, if the drainage is good.

Mulch with organic materials, or small rocks or gravel. Using compost for mulch, with a light application every few years, provides an opportunity to enrich the soil.

BLOOM

Short stems covered with dark-green leaves elongate in early summer. The bud stage is attractive as flowers form just above the foliage. Rosy-purple flowers in clusters open at the top of six-inch stems and hold their color for several weeks.

New growth emerges as flowering fades, and these stems may also form flowers in the same season. There will be fewer blossoms in this second wave of bloom.

Fading flower stalks are still attractive as they mature into seedheads. I do not remove them until midwinter, though if I did I might get more flowers in late summer.

Stems are short, but *Teucrium* x *lucidrys* 'Prostratum' could be used as a cut flower for small arrangements.

Butterflies and honeybees are attracted to this plant.

SEASONAL INTEREST

Teucrium x *lucidrys* 'Prostratum' is an outstanding evergreen groundcover for year-round interest. Fresh growth in spring is a highlight in my rock garden. All stages of flowering, from bud, to bloom, to seed, are attractive and interesting.

In winter, the dark-green foliage is one of the more outstanding features in my rock garden.

COMPANION PLANTS AND LANDSCAPE USE

Because of its vigorous growth, prostrate germander should be given space to spread. In the rock garden, rocks may be inserted into the soil to define its limits.

Use *Teucrium* x *lucidrys* 'Prostratum' as a small or large-scale groundcover. One-gallon plants may be planted two feet apart, and with good soil preparation will cover the designated area in one year. Because it grows so densely, it excludes light for weed seeds to germinate.

With its dark-green foliage and tolerance of low irrigation, prostrate germander has companions among the more xeriphitic groundcovers: *Cerastium* (snow-in-summer), *Stachys* (lamb's ears), *Cotoneaster* 'Tom Thumb', and *Antennaria dioica* (pussy toes).

Since it also tolerates more frequent irrigation, it may be combined beautifully with the green-leafed thymes. Flowers may be color echoes of the same or similar hues in pink, to rosy-pink, to purple. Foliage of thyme is finer with a broad range of green to offer contrast to the prostrate germander.

Erigeron karvinskianus (Santa Barbara daisy) is a lovely companion.

This is a good container plant but will need to be repotted every few years to reinvigorate its growth.

Teucrium x *lucidrys* 'Prostratum' is an attractive edging for a walkway, or as a niche plant in a stone wall. It may even be used as an edging plant in a mixed border, though you may have to watch its spread.

PROPAGATION

Vegetative cuttings should be taken in spring before stems elongate into a blooming stage. Once creeping germander starts blooming, it becomes more difficult to find good terminal growth, but some cutting material may be available from the new shoots buried in all the flowers.

MAINTENANCE

VERY, VERY EASY! No maintenance is necessary. If you prefer the appearance of the shiny dark-green foliage to the interesting texture of the seed stalks, use hedge clippers and sheer back the plant after bloom fades.

Teucrium x *lucidrys* 'Prostratum'

Thymus praecox ssp. *arcticus*

THYMUS

Thymus is another genus in the family *Lamiaceae (Labiatae)* which includes *Teucrium, Prunella, Lamium, Lamiastrum,* and *Mentha* (mint). Some 300 to 400 species of *Thymus* are within this genus of perennial herbs from Europe and Asia.

These evergreen and evergray groundcovers are invaluable in the landscape, and all are deer-resistant.

DESCRIPTION

Thymes vary considerably in leaf form and color, spreading habit, bloom color, and use in the landscape.

Thymus cherlerioides (silver needle thyme): A thyme for full sun, the silver needle thyme is one of my favorites. Trailing stems grow close to the ground. They are densely covered with tiny, fuzzy, gray-green leaves giving the plant an overall effect of gray. Height is under two inches, and spread to two to three feet. In late spring and early summer, multiple pink flowers open in the center area of the plant. The new growth of trailing branches has no flowers.

Thymus citriodorus (lemon thyme): *Thymus citriodorus* includes the species lemon thyme, which is an excellent culinary herb with a lemon flavor. Dark-green foliage is strongly scented and may have yellow variegation. Lemon thyme grows in a mound with a one-foot height and two-foot spread. It may need to be sheared back periodically to maintain vigor. Flowers are pink in early summer.

Also included in the species is the cultivar *Thymus citriodorus* 'Aureus' (golden lemon thyme), which has a similar growth habit and bloom, but more gold in the foliage. This is a good choice for partial shade.

Thymus 'Doone Valley' (Doone Valley or Doone's Valley thyme): This is a very attractive, low, mounding thyme with dark-green leaves during the summer and some golden variegation in spring and fall. Leaves have a slight rust tint in cold winters. Height is four to six inches and spread to two feet. Bloom is sparse, with pink flowers in early summer.

Thymus glabrescens (loveyanus thyme): Loveyanus thyme is one of the most vigorous of all the species I have grown. The leaves are·larger than other species, fuzzy and gray-green. Spread is very rapid to four feet with trailing stems to one foot or more. Flowering is heavy in summer and into fall with lavender-pink flowers held just above the foliage. This is a very beautiful groundcover for sunny gardens.

Thymus herba-barona (caraway thyme): Caraway thyme is the first thyme to bloom in my garden in spring, its lavender-rose flowers almost covering the delicate foliage in spring. The appearance of this rapidly spreading thyme is delicate and trailing, with tiny dark-green leaves spaced one-half inch apart along wiry reddish stems. Leaves are highly scented and may be used for cooking. Growth is close to the ground to four inches in height and two to three feet in spread.

Thymus heretus (heretus thyme): Heretus thyme is similar to caraway thyme in appearance, with tiny pointed leaves along reddish (but not wiry) stems, and heavy bloom in spring. Its height and spread are similar. Flowers are pink and leaves are spaced closer, giving it a fine but dense appearance. Leaves are not scented.

Thymus nitidus **(nitens thyme):** Nitens thyme is classified as a subspecies of *Thymus Richardii* in "Hortus Third". The specimen I purchased with this name is low-growing to a six-inch height and two-foot spread, with pink flowers in early summer.

Thymus praecox: This group of thymes includes several low-growing cultivars:

T. p. **'Albus' (white moss thyme)** has tiny, white flowers in clusters on one-inch stalks, nestling the flowers into the foliage. Tiny bright-green leaves grow closely on short, running stems, forming a dense mat under three inches in height. This is a beauty!

Thymus praecox **ssp.** ***arcticus*** **(*T. britannicus*) (Britannicus thyme)** is a subspecies with gray foliage and attractive growth habit. It is a strong spreader to three feet, with a low, dense growth under ten inches. Gray leaves are slightly fuzzy and highly scented (lemon and mint?). Flowers are light lavender-pink.

T. p. **'Elfin' ('Elfin' thyme, dwarf 'Elfin' thyme)** is a slowly spreading and mounding thyme. It is three inches in height, and may spread to one foot, with a light bloom of pink flowers close to the dark-green foliage. Leaves are very tiny, growing densely. This cultivar is more mounding than flat.

T. p. **'Hall's Woolly' ('Hall's Woolly' thyme)** is an attractive cultivar and a rapid spreader. Leaves are small, gray-green, with fine hairs covering the foliage. Bloom is prolific, with pink flowers in early summer. Height is under three inches, with a spread to two to three feet.

T. p. **'Pink Chintz' ('Pink Chintz' thyme)** grows very low and creeping, to a height under two inches and a spread to two feet. Fuzzy foliage is delicate and dark-green. Light-pink flowers open close to the foliage in summer.

Thymus pseudolanuginosus (*Thymus praecox arcticus* 'Lanuginosus') (woolly thyme) has fuzzy, tiny foliage with gray-green leaves growing closely together, forming a low, thick, and slightly mounding hilly mat. Leaves may change to pink tones in cold winters. This species rarely blooms, but when it does it has only a few tiny pink flowers.

Thymus pseudolanuginosus

Thymus pulegioides is a species that includes several attractive subspecies and cultivars. *T. p.* (**Pennsylvania Dutch tea thyme**) is one of my favorites, with dark-green glossy leaves. Its flowers are pink, opening in summer. This is a thickly spreading and mounding thyme to one foot in height, and two to three feet in spread.

T. p. coccineus (*coconut thyme*) is an attractive low-growing subspecies of *Thymus pulegioides*. Foliage is dense, with mid-green leaves. Height is under four inches and spread to two to three feet. Bright-pink flowers open close to the foliage for several weeks in summer.

T. p. cv. (*oregano-scented thyme*) is a spreading thyme that may be used for culinary purposes. Dense, dark-green foliage is mounding to one foot in height, and spreading to two feet. Pink flowers open in summer.

Thymus serpyllum minus

Thymus serpyllum (**creeping red thyme**) and the subspecies *Thymus serpyllum minus* (**alpine thyme, dwarf creeping thyme**) are two of the tightest and lowest of the creeping thymes. The tiny dark-green leaves make a dense mat of foliage under one-inch height. Spread is eighteen to twenty-four inches.

Creeping red thyme has dark-pink flowers blooming for several months in summer. Trailing stems creep along the ground. It's very attractive!

Alpine thyme is a strong spreader but not as trailing as creeping red thyme. Pink flowers are sporadic, opening in sections of the foliage. Bloom continues through most of the summer months. This is one of my favorites.

Both are very attractive to bees and butterflies.

Thymus vulgaris **(common thyme)** is the thyme most often used for cooking. It is shrubby (one-foot height and spread) and better used as a specimen plant for the rock garden or an edging plant, than a groundcover.

The species also includes named cultivars with variations of growth habit, leaf color, and bloom. All are more upright than spreading, with woody growth more typical of subshrubs.

T. v. 'Argenteus' (silver thyme): This is a thyme for full sun. The leaves are silvery-green with white variegation. In cold weather, there is a leaf color change to rose. Flowers in early summer are pink. Silver thyme grows to one foot in height and two to three feet in spread. Growth is woody but mounding.

T. v. 'Italian Oregano' ('Italian Oregano' thyme) has small, gray-green leaves that have an oregano scent, and multiple pink flowers in summer. This cultivar is very pretty in bloom. Height and spread are one foot, with upright woody growth.

T. v. 'Orange Balsam' ('Orange Balsam' thyme) is similar to 'Italian Oregano', with small, gray-green leaves on upright stems that have a citrus flavor. Light-pink flowers in summer are not as profuse as the blossoms of 'Italian Oregano'.

Note: There are five other thymes that I have grown, none of which has been accurately identified as a particular species. Their common names are noted as follows:

Lavender thyme is a very unusual and uncommon thyme. Light-green slender leaves are highly aromatic. This thyme does not do well in full hot sun. Flowers are pale lavender-pink in early summer. Lavender thyme is a low-grower, under two inches. It is also much smaller than most of the other species, spreading to little more than one foot.

Lemon frost thyme is a thyme with bright-green foliage and the scent of lemon when crushed. It is under six inches in height and two feet in spread. This is a very attractive low spreader that blooms with pink flowers in early summer.

Lime thyme, occasionally classified as *Thymus x citriodorus,* is a thyme with bright-green foliage, similar mounding habit, with growth under six inches in height, and a two-foot spread. My six-year-old specimens have not bloomed.

Mint thyme has tiny dark-green and slightly fuzzy leaves that grow close to the ground, under two inches in height. Spread is strong to two feet. The pink flowers open in profusion in late spring.

Reiter's thyme has tiny, pointed, dark-green leaves growing closely on stems trailing along the ground. Stems root as they spread. Bloom is outstanding, with dark-pink flowers for several weeks in late spring. Height is under three inches, and spread two to three feet.

CULTURAL REQUIREMENTS

Thymus cherlerioides

Thymus is a genus with many species that will do well in the coldest regions of the mountain and intermountain western United States. Winter hardiness may vary from microclimate to microclimate even within the same geographical region.

Thymes with gray leaves should be grown in full sun. *Thymus cherlerioides, Thymus praecox arcticus,* and *Thymus glabrescens* require the least amount of irrigation and are the most tolerant of a hot southern or western exposure. Irrigation once every three weeks is sufficient.

Most of the thymes described have green leaves of varying shades. All will tolerate full sun or very light shade. Those with light-green leaves or variegation will tolerate more shade.

Soil should not be rich, but must be amended with organic compost and phosphorus. Avoid the use of any fertilizer high in nitrogen. Add oyster shell in acidic soils to release all the nutrients. *Thymus* is a genus that does well in rocky soils.

As noted, gray-leafed thymes are xeriphitic, requiring water only once every few weeks. In a sunny exposure, and soil with very good drainage, they may tolerate irrigation more frequently. Green-leafed thymes prefer deep watering once every two weeks. They, too, may be watered more frequently (once a week) in well-drained soil.

Mulches may be of organic materials low in nitrogen, small rocks, or gravel.

BLOOM

Thymus herba-barona

Clusters of flowers typical of the mint family open beginning in late spring and continuing through the summer months.

Thymus pulegioides coccineus and *Thymus serpyllum minus* are the longest-blooming thymes. *Thymus herba-barona* is an early bloomer and *Thymus glabrescens* is a late bloomer.

Some are heavier bloomers as noted, and a few have sparse flowering or none at all.

Thymes do not need deadheading, though shearing faded flowers may make the plant appearance more tidy. Usually new growth will cover the faded flowers.

All thyme flowers are very attractive to bees and butterflies. A wide variety of pollinating insects visits these blossoms.

SEASONAL INTEREST

As evergreens and evergrays, all species of *Thymus* are beautiful ground-covers, edgers, and specimen plants year-round in the garden. Extending bloom for many weeks from spring through summer, *Thymus* supplies a long season of color.

COMPANION PLANTS AND LANDSCAPE USE

Thymus glabrescens

With attention to their eventual spread and height, gardeners may choose any one of the *Thymus* for a large or small-scale groundcover. Space according to spread.

Between stepping stones, even in high-traffic areas, *Thymus serpyllum minus* is the perfect choice.

The most vigorous and largest spreading thyme, *Thymus glabrescens* (loveyanus thyme) and *Thymus praecox arcticus* (Britannicus thyme) are perfect choices for a weed-suppressing groundcover in full sun. They thrive even in a western exposure and on a slope. Companion plants for these xeriphitic thymes include *Santolina* (lavender cotton), *Cotoneaster*, *Origanum* species (oregano), *Rosmarinus* (rosemary), *Verbena rigida,* and *Stachys* (lamb's ears). Refer to Appendix 3.

The trailing thymes are also very beautiful in containers or spilling over a rock wall. Remember that their vigorous growth may cover the rocks. In my garden, I have stacked cinder blocks at varying heights to create planters for thyme. They have completely covered most of the cinder blocks, and are attractive in every season.

Thymes are certainly good companions to one another. Throughout this volume I have recommended them as evergreen companions for several other groundcovers or rock garden perennials.

I frequently use thymes as evergreen edging plants for flower borders and along walkways.

Grow *Thymus* species and cultivars near your vegetable garden to attract beneficial insects and honeybees.

Erigeron karvinskianus (Santa Barbara daisy) is a beautiful summer-flowering companion. *Teucrium cossonii* ssp. *majoricum* (trailing germander) looks wonderful growing adjacent to any of the *Thymus* with green foliage. Watering this pair would need to be once every two weeks (for the *Thymus*). The trailing germander will tolerate this irrigation schedule if it is growing in sun, in soil with good drainage.

PROPAGATION

Vegetative propagation is very easy. Trailing stems provide two-inch cuttings, and may even root as they trail over mulch, providing divisions to lift.

Take vegetative cuttings from April through November.

Thymus with very tight growth habit ('Elfin' thyme, lavender thyme) are easiest to propagate from divisions taken in late fall, winter in mild climates, or early spring.

Thymus vulgaris, and the cultivars within this species with a woody growth habit, need to be propagated by cuttings since growth habit does not provide material for divisions. Sometimes layering will work with cultivars of this species by stapling (with a landscape staple) a woody branch into the mulch. Once the branch is rooted, it may be cut from the parent plant.

MAINTENANCE

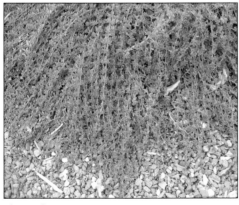

VERY, VERY EASY! No maintenance is necessary. If a plant dies out in the center, it is usually an indication of inadequate drainage in winter. When this happens, prune out the dead growth and apply a mulch of compost. New growth should soon cover the missing portion.

Thymus heretus

Verbena rigida

Verbena rigida (V. venosa)

Verbena rigida is an excellent groundcover or edging plant, especially for a low-irrigation garden in full sun. It is very vigorous, spreading by stolons, and may be too invasive for small gardens. On southern and western slopes, it adds lots of purple all summer. Refer to Appendix 3 of this volume for a list of companion plants.

For details, refer to "Deer in My Garden, Vol. 1".

Veronica liwanensis

Veronica
(speedwell)

Trailing and creeping speedwells are excellent deer-resistant groundcovers and specimen plants for the rock garden. All are low in their growth habit. In my garden, the deer have eaten all the taller *Veronicas,* so this genus was not incorporated into "Deer in My Garden, Vol. 1", except in the appendix that listed deer-resistant edging perennials.

I am pleased to include low-growing *Veronicas* in this volume, especially because the deer have allowed me to grow so many species. *Veronica alpina* 'Alba' is an attractive low-growing speedwell that I'm now testing in the garden. Occasionally the deer have eaten its white flower stalks (which are more similar to the taller *Veronicas),* but they have not damaged the dark-green leaves that grow in attractive rosettes.

DESCRIPTION

Veronica Allionii is a rare species of semi-evergreen *Veronica* from the Swiss Alps. Dark, trailing stems are delicate, to one foot or less, with tiny dark-green leaves. In early spring, cobalt-blue flowers open for three to four weeks. Height is under six inches and spread is eighteen inches or less.

Veronica liwanensis is the most vigorous grower of the species described here. Tiny, round bright-green leaves grow on long, creeping stems that root as they trail if they are not climbing through neighboring plants. Height is under two inches, and spread is as far as you allow it to grow. This evergreen looks delicate, but is amazingly strong both in its growth habit and its tolerance for a variety of exposures. Periwinkle-blue flowers open in profusion for several weeks in spring into early summer.

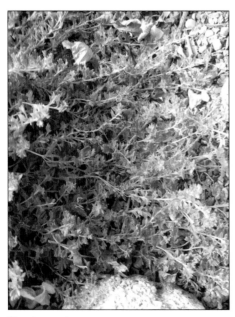

Veronica pectinata

Veronica pectinata is native to the Mediterranean. Another low-growing evergreen *Veronica,* this species spreads quickly, forming a low mat (under three inches in height) of trailing stems with gray-green, somewhat fuzzy leaves. Stems root as they grow, adding strength to the spread. Small, deep-blue flowers open along each trailing stem for several weeks in early to midsummer.

Veronica repens has the tightest growth habit of all the species that are low-growers. This evergreen species is under one inch in height, and will spread to one foot or more. This is the only one I would use between stepping stones, because the other species and cultivars would spread too quickly and cover the stones. Tiny bright-green leaves grow densely. Singular, pale lavender-blue flowers are tiny, in clusters within the foliage in spring.

Veronica umbrosa '**Georgia Blue**' is a trailing and mounding semi-evergreen *Veronica* with a height to one foot and a spread to three feet. Its trailing stems and small flowers are delicate like the other *Veronicas.* Bright-blue flowers open in early spring, almost covering the dark-green foliage.

Veronica 'Waterperry Blue'

Veronica '**Waterperry Blue**' (*V.* '**Waterperry**') is the longest-blooming of all the trailing and creeping *Veronicas.* This semi-evergreen cultivar is another low-grower, under six inches in height. Typical of the trailing *Veronicas,* its dark-brown stems are delicate. Dark-green leaves are rounded, with a serrated edge and bronze tint, spaced apart along the stems. Spread is two to three feet. Light-blue flowers have dark-blue markings and begin opening in spring, when bloom is heaviest. A few flowers continue to open throughout the summer months.

CULTURAL REQUIREMENTS

All the *Veronica* species will take considerable winter cold. The strongest evergreens are *Veronica liwanensis, Veronica pectinata,* and *Veronica repens.* If they show any damage following winter, they quickly recover in spring. Others are described as semi-evergreen because they may be dormant in cold winters.

Most *Veronicas* prefer some afternoon shade in my hot-summer climate in the foothills of the Sierra Nevada mountains. *Veronica* 'Waterperry Blue' and *Veronica umbrosa* 'Georgia Blue' will tolerate full sun if they are watered once a week in the heat of the summer.

In garden climates with fog or cloud cover, all species of *Veronica* will grow and bloom well in partial shade or full sun.

Soil should be fertile, improved with organic compost and phosphorus. Use oyster shell in acidic soils to release nutrients. *Veronicas* grow easily in rocky fertile soil.

Regular irrigation once a week in the heat of summer is ideal for most of the species, grown in full sun or partial shade. *Veronica pectinata* does well with less water. Its gray-green leaves are a clue to its tolerance of lower irrigation.

Mulches should be of organic materials and may be renewed each year to add nutrients and maintain optimal moisture retention.

BLOOM

See Description for individual differences between cultivars and species. Flowers are small, usually little more than one-quarter inch. Color is strong, except for *Veronica repens,* and plants in bloom are very attractive.

A long season of blooming is most typical of *Veronica* 'Waterperry Blue'.

Flowers fade without any need for deadheading. They disappear into the foliage.

SEASONAL INTEREST

Three of the species of *Veronica* are evergreen: *Veronica liwanensis, Veronica pectinata,* and *Veronica repens.* These are attractive year-round.

Other species are semi-evergreen, and begin strong growth in late winter. The foliage of all the species is a good addition to the partial-shade garden.

The sequence of bloom from early spring into midsummer provides a long season of color when all the cultivars are grown in the garden.

COMPANION PLANTS AND LANDSCAPE USE

Because I am irrigating my rock garden only once every two weeks in the heat of the summer, *Veronica pectinata* is the only species I can grow there.

A rock garden with more frequent irrigation would be a good place for specimens of any of the species. Remember that *Veronica liwanensis* is an aggressive spreader, and even a good choice for a large-scale groundcover in partial sun.

Use *Veronica repens* between stepping stones since its growth is more compact than the other species.

Trailing speedwells make good choices for planting above a rock wall. *Veronica Allionii*, *Veronica* 'Waterperry Blue', and *Veronica umbrosa* 'Georgia Blue' will spill over the wall without covering much of the rocks. 'Waterperry Blue' and 'Georgia Blue' have enough height that if the soil behind the wall settles a few inches, they will still grow up and over the rocks.

Use *Veronica* species as edging plants for a border or along a walkway.

The evergreen *Veronica liwanensis* will spill over the rocks in a wall and creep through the crevices, covering more of the wall. Its delicate appearance and bright-green foliage are beautiful against the rocks.

The fine foliage of *Veronica liwanensis* has several good companions among larger-leaved perennials for partial shade: *Digitalis* species (foxglove), *Rubus calycinoides* (creeping raspberry), and any species of *Helleborus* (hellebore). This is a very vigorous groundcover for the irrigated shade garden.

All the trailing species of *Veronica* are beautiful plants for containers. *Veronica liwanensis* is as beautiful out of bloom as it is when sweet little blue flowers accent its delicate foliage.

Arabis procurrens (rockcress) is a good companion for all the *Veronicas* except *Veronica liwanensis*. Both grow close to the ground, and the rockcress would disappear under the vigorous growth of the speedwell.

PROPAGATION

All the *Veronica* species are very easy from vegetative cuttings taken during the growing season.

Divisions may also be made in late fall, during winter in mild climates, or in early spring. The earliest bloomer, *Veronica umbrosa* 'Georgia Blue', should be divided in late fall so the next year's bloom will not be affected. Cut back the current season's growth before dividing.

MAINTENANCE

VERY EASY! No deadheading is necessary because the flowers fade into the foliage.

The following species should be cut back to the crown during the winter (or in late fall if you plan to divide them): *Veronica Allionii*, *Veronica* 'Waterperry Blue', and *Veronica umbrosa* 'Georgia Blue'.

Renew mulch on an annual basis, if possible, with a very light application of compost.

Viola labradorica

VIOLA

Violets have been hybridized for larger leaves and larger flowers, and the deer are very grateful. It is the smaller, sweet violet of poems and old gardens that the deer usually will not eat. The only time they have been bothered by the deer in my garden was when the violets were responding to the compost I had added with lusher growth.

Viola labradorica
(Labrador violet)

This sweet little violet is evergreen in milder climates, and deciduous in very cold climates. It grows natively in Canada, Greenland, and in the northeastern United States.

DESCRIPTION

Small dark-green leaves are about one-half inch in length. The cultivar with purple flowers has leaves shaded with purple. Height is under four inches and spread as far as space allows.

Viola labradorica spreads by seed and by runners extending above-ground from the edges of the plant.

Purple or pink flowers open in late spring.

CULTURAL REQUIREMENTS

See Viola odorata. Viola labradorica is very tolerant of full sun, even in my hot-summer climate. It does not do well in deep shade.

BLOOM

Flowers of one cultivar are light-purple, and of another a rosy-pink. Both are small, barely more than one-fourth inch. Bloom begins after Viola odorata, late spring into early summer.

Developing seed capsules will spread seed, sometimes several feet away from the parent plants.

SEASONAL INTEREST

See Viola odorata.

COMPANION PLANTS AND LANDSCAPE USE

See Viola odorata. Because of its low growth, Viola labradorica is an outstanding plant between stepping stones. It survives even with frequent traffic from people and dogs.

PROPAGATION

See Viola odorata.

MAINTENANCE

See *Viola odorata.*

Viola odorata
(sweet violet)

DESCRIPTION

Viola odorata

My description must begin with the first winter I spent in this old homestead garden. Hundreds of small purple violets, sweetly fragrant, began opening in December and continued for several weeks.

Dark-green leaves are slightly heart-shaped, growing from the crown at the end of very short stems. Leaves face outward and flowers form on two-inch stalks from the center of the plant. This is an attractive evergreen perennial groundcover with a tufted growth habit.

Plants spread in three ways: the crown becomes larger, runners spread forming new plants, and the seed settling into the mulch will germinate the following season. Roots are not deep.

Height is under six inches, and spread will be as far as garden conditions allow.

CULTURAL REQUIREMENTS

Viola odorata is an evergreen perennial hardy to very cold climates, and tolerant of summer heat. It grows natively in Europe, North Africa, and Asia.

In coastal areas with summer fog and mild temperatures, sweet violet will grow in full sun. Partial shade is a better exposure in hot-summer climates. *Viola odorata* will grow and bloom well in partial shade in all climates. In my gardening area, in the foothills of the Sierra Nevada, summer light is very bright and violets do well even in deep shade. For optimal growth and bloom soil should be fertile, enriched with organic compost and phosphorus. Add oyster shell in acidic soils. Concentrate soil preparation in the upper six inches. *Viola odorata* is somewhat drought-tolerant. There are plants growing in the shade on the north side of my house that receive rainfall in winter, but no summer irrigation except when there is a very rare rain. In these dry conditions, growth is not as vigorous and bloom is far less than in my irrigated garden. Water sweet violets once every one to two weeks.

Mulch with organic materials while plants are blooming to provide a bed for the tiny seed that will germinate next winter and early spring.

BLOOM

Fragrant purple violets begin blooming in my garden in December and continue for two months. In January an early white violet opens, followed by a white with purple markings in the center. Next in the bloom sequence is a magenta, followed by a later white, and finally another deep-pink violet in May. The long bloom sequence of this edible and scented flower delights my grandchildren.

Flowers do not need to be deadheaded. Let the seed mature to self-sow.

SEASONAL INTEREST

Viola odorata is a beautiful evergreen plant year-round. A long season of bloom is possible from December through May by growing several cultivars.

For me, one of the most interesting times to enjoy violets is in late winter when seed is germinating, and the tiny plants are growing adjacent to the parent plants.

COMPANION PLANTS AND LANDSCAPE USE

Viola odorata is such a vigorously spreading groundcover that it consumes the area in which it grows. Bulbs may be planted before the violets establish. *Leucojum aestivum* and *Narcissus* species are beautiful companions to violets in partial shade.

Sweet violets are an attractive groundcover naturalized under ornamental shrubs or small trees: *Choisya ternata* (Mexican orange), *Lonicera nitida* (box honeysuckle), and *Magnolia stellata* (star magnolia) are good companions.

In low-traffic areas, sweet violets may be used between stepping stones. Along a walkway in partial shade, they are a perfect evergreen edging plant.

In small containers, *Viola odorata* is a charming addition to a small garden. Remember that the seed may spread into your garden.

This vigorous perennial may be used as a groundcover for small or large areas. Restraining its spread in a small garden may be necessary if it is invading other treasured perennials. For this reason, use larger perennials such as species of *Helleborus* (hellebore), and *Euphorbia* x *martinii* (spurge).

Ornamental grasses for partial shade are good companions: *Hakonechloa macra* 'Aureola' (Japanese forest grass), *Chasmanthium latifolium* (spangle grass), *Carex glauca* (blue sedge), and *Molinia caerulea* (moor grass). Violets spreading into these mounding grasses are an attractive contrast, in leaf form and color.

In my garden, violets have spread into my perennial border. The tall perennials shade them in summer. These herbaceous perennials are cut back to the crown at the end of fall. The sweet violets become the focus of attention during the winter months, before perennials begin growth in early spring. For this companion planting, I use the purple and early white violets because the growth of the perennials begins in March, and I don't want the violets to be lost from view.

PROPAGATION

Seed capsules may be gathered when mature and seed spread where plants are desired. *Viola odorata* will also self-sow. Many seeds will germinate if they fall into a mulch of compost.

If mulch around mature plants needs to be renewed, spread it while plants are blooming. At that time, seed germinating from the previous season's blooms will produce young seedlings. Avoid covering the seedlings, but spread enough compost to provide a seed bed for next year's crop.

Young seedlings may be lifted in sections and replanted. Mature plants may also be divided in late fall.

MAINTENANCE

VERY, VERY EASY! No maintenance is required. Mulch may be renewed (see Propagation), but does not need to be done every year if good soil preparation has been done in the beginning.

Zauschneria californica

ZAUSCHNERIA

Zauschneria californica (Epilobium californica)
(California fuchsia, hummingbird trumpet)

This species for mild climates includes several cultivars that range in height from six inches to a few feet. Winter hardiness varies. A ground-cover for large-scale areas, this is another tough perennial for western and southern slopes in full sun. Refer to Appendix 3 for companions.

Refer to "Deer in My Garden, Vol. 1" for details.

APPENDIX 1

GROUNDCOVERS & EDGERS BY COMMON NAME

alyssum, perennial — *Alyssum montanum*

angel's hair — *Artemisia schmidtiana*

baby's breath, creeping — *Gypsophila repens*

beardtongue — *Penstemon* species

bellflower, Serbian — *Campanula poscharskyana*

bishop's weed — *Aegopodium podagraria*

blue star creeper — *Pratia pedunculata (Isotoma fluviatilis, Laurentia fluviatilis)*

chamomile, garden or Russian — *Chamaemelum nobile (Anthemis nobilis)*

California fuchsia — *Zauschneria (Epilobium)*

carpet bugle — *Ajuga reptans*

catmint — *Nepeta* species

cat's-foot — *Antennaria dioica* 'Rosea'

cinquefoil, creeping — *Potentilla canadensis*

cotoneaster, dwarf cranberry — *Cotoneaster apiculatus* 'Tom Thumb'

cotoneaster, rockspray — *Cotoneaster microphyllus*

creeping jenny — *Lysimachia nummularia*

dead nettle — *Lamium galeobdolon (Lamiastrum galeobdolon)* & *Lamium maculatum*

fleabane — *Erigeron karvinskianus*

forget-me-not — *Myosotis scorpioides*

geranium — *Geranium sanguineum* & *G. x cantabrigiense*

germander, prostrate — *Teucrium x lucidrys* 'Prostratum' *(T. x chamaedrys* 'Compactum')

germander, trailing	*Teucrium cossonii* ssp. *majoricum* (*T. cussonii majoricum, T. majoricum*)
germander, upright	*Teucrium* x *lucidrys*
ginger, wild	*Asarum caudatum*
goldenrod	*Solidago* 'Golden Baby'
goutweed	*Aegopodium podagraria*
heal-all	*Prunella vulgaris*
holly grape, creeping	*Mahonia repens*
hummingbird trumpet	*Zauschneria (Epilobium) californica*
ice plant, hardy	*Delosperma nubigenum* 'Lesotho'
iris, winter	*Iris unguicularis*
Kenilworth ivy	*Cymbalaria muralis*
lady's mantle	*Alchemilla mollis*
lamb's ears, lamb's tongue)	*Stachys byzantina* (*S. lanata, S. olympica*)
lavender cotton	*Santolina*
lavender, dwarf white English	*Lavandula angustifolia nana* 'Alba'
manzanita, creeping	*Arctostaphylos uva-ursi*
moneywort	*Lysimachia nummularia*
moss pink	*Phlox subulata*
Mrs. Robb's bonnet	*Euphorbia amygdaloides* ssp. *robbiae*
oregano	*Origanum* species
penstemon	*Penstemon* species
phlox, creeping	*Phlox subulata*
pinks	*Dianthus* species
'Powis Castle' (*A.* 'Powys Castle')	*Artemisia* cultivar
pussy toes	*Antennaria dioica* 'Rosea'
raspberry, creeping	*Rubus calycinoides*
rockcress	*Arabis procurrens*
rockcress, variegated	*Arabis Ferdinandi-Coburgi* 'Variegata'
rockcress, wall	*Arabis caucasica* (*A. albida*)
rosemary, trailing	*Rosmarinus officinalis* 'Lockwood de Forest' ('Lockwoodii', 'Forestii', 'Santa Barbara')
rupturewort	*Herniaria glabra*
sage, common	*Salvia officinalis*
Santa Barbara daisy	*Erigeron karvinskianus*

'Sea Foam'	*Artemisia versicolor*
self-heal	*Prunella vulgaris*
snow-in-summer	*Cerastium Biebersteinii (C. biebersteinii) & Cerastium tomentosum*
speedwell	*Veronica* species
spirea, alpine	*Spiraea japonica* 'Alpina' ('Nana')
spurge, cypress	*Euphorbia cyparissias*
spurge, wood	*Euphorbia amygdaloides* ssp. *robbiae*
sundrops	*Oenothera tetragona*
sweet woodruff	*Galium odoratum*
tansy	*Tanacetum densum* ssp. *amani*
thyme	*Thymus species*
tickseed, threadleaf	*Coreopsis verticillata* 'Moonbeam'
verbena, vervain	*Verbena rigida (V. venosa)*
violet, Labrador	*Viola labradorica*
violet, sweet	*Viola odorata*
woolly betony	*Stachys byzantina (S. lanata, S. olympica)*
wormwood	*Artemisia* species
yarrow, common	*Achillea millefolium*
yarrow, creeping	*Achillea* x 'King Edward'
yarrow, Greek	*Achillea ageratifolia*
yarrow, silvery	*Achillea Clavennae*
yarrow, woolly	*Achillea tomentosa*
yellow archangel	*Lamium galeobdolon (Lamiastrum galeobdolon)*

APPENDIX 2

MORE DEER-RESISTANT "GROUND-COVERS" FROM LARGE TO SMALL

Section 1: The ornamental shrubs & subshrubs that serve as large groundcovers (to be described in Vol. 3 of "Deer in My Garden"):

Baccharis pilularis 'Pigeon Point' & 'Twin Peaks' (dwarf coyote brush)

Berberis x *stenophylla* (rosemary barberry)

Buddleia (Buddleja) alternifolia (fountain butterfly bush)

Carpenteria californica (bush anemone)

Choisya ternata (Mexican orange)

Cotoneaster buxifolius

Daphne odora (sweet daphne)

Elaeagnus pungens & *E.* x *ebbingei* (silverberry)

Erica x *darleyensis* (heath)

Grevillea 'Canberra Gem' ('Canberra')

Hypericum androsaemum (purple St. Johnswort)

Hypericum x *moserianum* (gold flower)

Ilex vomitoria 'Nana' or 'Stokes' (dwarf Yaupon holly)

Juniperus species (juniper)

Lonicera nitida 'Maigruen' (box honeysuckle)

Mahonia aquifolium 'Compacta' (dwarf Oregon grape)

Nandina filamentosa (threadleaf heavenly bamboo)

Pinus mugo (mugho pine)

Sarcococca confusa & *S. ruscifolia* (sweet vanilla plant)

Viburnum davidii (David's viburnum)

Note: *Cistus* species (rockrose) and *Ceanothus* are not deer-resistant although they are on several "deer-resistant" plant lists.

Section 2: The smallest of groundcovers:

Aethionema armenum 'Warley Rose' (*A. x warleyense*) (stonecress, Persian candytuft)

Alyssum tortuosum (alpine alyssum)

Armeria maritima (sea thrift)

Centaurea stricta (alpine cornflower)

Erinus alpinus (alpine erinus, alpine liver-balsam, fairy foxglove)

Erysimum helveticum (alpine wallflower, Swiss treacle-mustard)

Gypsophila cerastioides (mouse-ears)

Lychnis Flos-Jovis (dwarf rabbit's ears)

Saponaria pumilio (alpine soapwort)

Scleranthus uniflorus (four-flowered knamel)

Sedum album 'Athoum' (stonecrop)

Sedum album 'Faro Form' (stonecrop)

Sedum dasyphyllum (stonecrop)

Sedum sexangulare (tasteless stonecrop)

Silene acaulis (cushion pink, moss campion)

Silene alpestris

Silene schafta (moss campion)

Silene vulgaris ssp. *maritima* (bladder campion)

APPENDIX 3

GROUNDCOVERS FOR CHALLENGING LANDSCAPE SITUATIONS

Full-sun western & southern exposures, including slopes:

Achillea species

Alyssum montanum

Antennaria dioica 'Rosea'

Arctostaphylos uva-ursi

Artemisia species

Aubrieta deltoidea

Cerastium Biebersteinii
(C. biebersteinii) & *C. tomentosum*

Coreopsis verticillata 'Moonbeam'

Cotoneaster apiculatus 'Tom Thumb'
& *C. microphyllus*

Dianthus species

Erigeron karvinskianus

Gypsophila repens

Lavandula angustifolia nana 'Alba'

Mahonia repens

Nepeta species

Origanum species (except *O. vulgare*
'Aureum')

Phlox subulata

Rosmarinus officinalis
'Lockwood de Forest'

Salvia officinalis

Santolina species

Spiraea japonica 'Alpina'

Stachys byzantina

Tanacetum densum ssp. *amani*

Teucrium cossonii ssp. *majoricum* &
T. x lucidrys

Thymus species, gray-leafed only

Verbena rigida

Zauschneria (Epilobium)

Shade or partial shade in summer; sun or partial shade in winter:

Aegopodium podagraria

Alchemilla mollis

Asarum caudatum

Campanula poscharskyana

Cymbalaria muralis

Euphorbia amygdaloides ssp. robbiae

Galium odoratum

Geranium sanguineum &
G. x cantabrigiense

Herniaria glabra

Lamiastrum galeobdolon

Lamium maculatum 'Aureum', 'Pink Chablis', 'Pink Pewter', 'White Nancy' (the more silver or white on the leaf, the more shade it requires)

Lysimachia nummularia 'Aurea'

Mahonia repens

Myosotis scorpioides

Origanum vulgare 'Aureum'

Phlox subulata

Potentilla canadensis

Pratia pedunculata

Prunella vulgaris

Rubus calycinoides

Sarcococca hookerana humilis

Stachys byzantina

Vernonica Allionii, V. liwanensis & V. repens

Viola labradorica & V. odorata

Northern slopes: full or partial sun in summer; partial shade or reduced light in winter:

Ajuga reptans

Alchemilla mollis

Arabis procurrens

Aubrieta gracilis

Campanula poscharskyana

Chamaemelum nobile

Cotoneaster apiculatus 'Tom Thumb'

Delosperma nubigenum 'Lesotho'

Euphorbia amygdaloides ssp. robbiae

Euphorbia cyparissias

Galium odoratum

Herniaria glabra

Iris unguicularis

Lamium maculatum 'Roseum' & 'Album' (morning sun)

Lysimachia nummularia

Mahonia repens

Oenothera tetragona

Origanum vulgare 'Aureum'

Phlox subulata

Potentilla canadensis

Prunella vulgaris

Rosmarinus officinalis 'Lockwood de Forest'

Rubus calycinoides

Sarcococca hookerana humilis

Solidago 'Golden Baby'

Spiraea japonica 'Alpina'

Stachys byzantina

Teucrium x lucidrys & T. x l. 'Prostratum'

Thymus species, green-leafed only

Veronica Allionii, V. 'Waterperry Blue' & V. umbrosa 'Georgia Blue'

Viola labradorica & V. odorata

INDEX

A

G

Galanthus 13, 21, 44, 110, 133, 139
   G. elwesii 136
Galium odoratum 97; photo, 97
Garden chamomile 76
Geranium 97, 191
   G. sanguineum 'Cedric Morris' 97;
   photo, 97; 191, 197
   G. x cantabrigiense 'Biokovo' 97, 191,
   197
Germander 73, 120, 144, 158, 161-169,
178, 192
Giant feather grass 115
Giant snowdrop 136
Ginger 58, 59, 60, 69, 151, 192
Gold common oregano 124
Gold flower 194
Gold sedge 87
Goldenrod 139
Goutweed 27-29
Grama grass 99, 130
Green lavender cotton 54
Grevillea 194
   'Canberra' 194
   'Canberra Gem' 194
Gypsophila 13, 65, 94, 97-99, 191
   G. cerastioides 65, 195
   G. repens 13, 94, 97-99, 191, 196
      'Alba' 19, 98, 110, 180
      'Rosea' 13

H

Hakonechloa 87, 109, 151
   H. macro 'Aureola' 87, 189
Hardy ice plant 88-89
Heath 194
Helianthus 139
   H. maximilianii 139
Helictotrichon sempervirens 56, 75, 144
Hellebore 42, 69, 87, 184, 189
Helleborus 42, 69, 87, 109, 184, 189
Herniaria 100-102
   H. alpina 100

H. glabra 100-102, 112, 192, 197
Hummingbird trumpet 190
Hutchinsia alpina 100, 197
Hypericum androsaemum 194
   H. x moserianum 194

I

Ice plant 87-89
Ilex vomitoria 194
   'Nana' 194
   'Stokes' 194
Impatiens 109
Iris 42, 69, 102, 192
   I. spuria 120
   I. unguicularis 42, 69, 102; photo, 102;
   192, 197
Isotoma 135-136; 191
   I. fluviatilis 135-136; 191

J

Japanese forest grass 87, 109, 189
Juniper 194
Juniperus 194

K

Kenilworth ivy 85-87, 192

L

Labiatae 170
Labrador violet 77, 186
Lady's mantle 33, 42, 192
Lamb's ears 83, 155-158, 164, 169, 177
Lamb's tongue 155
Lamiaceae 138, 167, 170
Lamiastrum 6, 69, 103-106, 157, 170,
193
   L. galeobdolon 69, 103-106; photo,
   103; 108, 109, 193
Lamium 103
   L. maculatum 6, 60, 87, 101, 106-110,
   138, 147, 151, 157, 167, 170, 191,
   193, 197
      'Album' 106-110 photo, 106; 107
      'Aureum' 106-110, 107
      'Beacon Silver' 107-110, 107
      'Chequers' 106-110, 107

Z

ORDER FORM

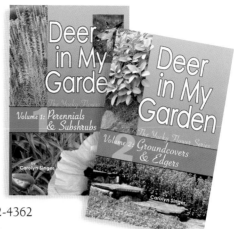

Telephone orders: Call (530) 272-4362

Email orders: orders@gardenwisdompress.com

Postal orders: Garden Wisdom Press, P.O. Box 992, Grass Valley CA 95945

NAME_____

ADDRESS _____

CITY _____STATE_____ZIP _____

TELEPHONE _____

EMAIL ADDRESS _____

Please send _____copies of Vol. 1 @ $19.95 .... _____

Please send _____copies of Vol. 2 @ $19.95 .... _____

Add CA sales tax @ 7.375% for all orders within CA .... _____

Indicate preferred shipping:

    U.S. Media Mail @ $2.40/book* .... _____

    U.S. Priority Mail @ $5.00/book .... _____

    Canada First Class @ $5.00/book** .... _____

*Add $2.00 to base shipping rate for each additional book .... _____

**Add $3.00 to base shipping rate for each additional book ...... _____

Total Due (check or money order).. _____

For payment thru PayPal, order online at **www.gardenwisdompress.com**

ORDER FORM

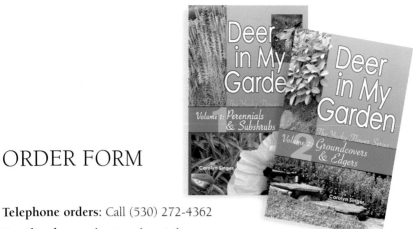

Telephone orders: Call (530) 272-4362

Email orders: orders@gardenwisdompress.com

Postal orders: Garden Wisdom Press, P.O. Box 992, Grass Valley CA 95945

NAME_____

ADDRESS _____

CITY _____STATE_____ZIP _____

TELEPHONE _____

EMAIL ADDRESS _____

Please send _____copies of Vol. 1 @ $19.95 .... _____

Please send _____copies of Vol. 2 @ $19.95 .... _____

Add CA sales tax @ 7.375% for all orders within CA .... _____

Indicate preferred shipping:

    U.S. Media Mail @ $2.40/book* .... _____

    U.S. Priority Mail @ $5.00/book .... _____

    Canada First Class @ $5.00/book** .... _____

*Add $2.00 to base shipping rate for each additional book .... _____

**Add $3.00 to base shipping rate for each additional book ...... _____

Total Due (check or money order).. _____

For payment thru PayPal, order online at **www.gardenwisdompress.com**